AN INTRODUCTION TO
SCULPTURE

From Its Origins to Today

By GUILLAUME JANNEAU
and SIMONE HOOG

 GOLDEN PRESS · NEW YORK

contents

Published in 1970 by Golden Press, New York, N.Y.,
a division of Western Publishing Company, Inc.
Copyright © 1970 by Editions des Deux Coqs d'Or, Paris,
and Mondadori-OGAM, Verona.
Printed in Italy

GOLDEN, GOLDEN ART GUIDE and GOLDEN PRESS
are trademarks of Western Publishing Company, Inc.

Library of Congress Catalog Card Number: 76–119565.

A GOLDEN ART GUIDE
This book is the fourth in the series
of Golden Art Guides. Others in the series include
ARCHITECTURE by Charles Rambert
PAINTING by Geneviève Monnier
MODERN PAINTING by Michel Hoog

Cover picture: *The Kiss*, Auguste Rodin, 1886,
Rodin Museum, Paris. (Photo Giraudon)
© by S.P.A.D.E.M., Paris, 1970.

the art of sculpture | 1

The art of sculpture—which involves carving hard materials or modelling soft ones into some definitive form—is one of man's easiest and simplest ways to express himself. Whereas painting requires elaborate techniques, a sculptor can simply shape clay with his hands, letting the sun harden it, or he can tackle harder materials with a cutting tool.

Sculptors can work in a wide variety of materials and make the most of their individual qualities. Furthermore, they work on almost any scale: a tiny carved ivory knife from Djebel-el-Arak is sculpture, as are the monumental glazed brick bas-reliefs of the palaces at Susa, and also Chinese bronzes and Sèvres porcelain figurines—all are pieces of sculpture.

Although engraved jewels and medals are customarily studied separately, as are small hammered, drawn, cast and engraved metal works, all these nonetheless can be considered as sculpture. It should be remembered that Jean Varin, one of the 17th century's greatest medallists, also excelled in making portrait busts, while Benvenuto Cellini produced exquisite jewellery with the same genius that he executed the famous *Perseus* now in Florence.

Nike of Samothrace, or **Winged Victory.** Marble, end of 3rd century B.C. Unearthed at Samothrace in 1863, this statue formerly decorated the prow of a votive ship. Louvre, Paris. (Normandy Photo)

MATERIALS AND TECHNIQUES

Modelling. The oldest and simplest sculptural technique is that of modelling, usually in a plastic substance such as soft clay. Originally, sculptors moulded material to the desired shape with their hands. Later such simple tools as roughing chisels and jointers were invented to remove excess clay. Then the finished product was either sun-dried or fired in a kiln: hence the name terra-cotta (baked earth) given to works made in this manner. Because of this material's fragility, a metal armature is also sometimes used.

Sun-dried or kiln-fired objects can remain unadorned, or may be painted various colours or coated with a vitreous glaze. The art of creating objects out of terra-cotta is called ceramics and includes both porous pottery (terra-cotta, faience) and impermeable pottery (stoneware, porcelain).

Hard materials and direct carving. Carving hard elements requires more elaborate tools, but these have changed very little over the centuries. The sculptor attacks the material directly. In order to fashion

it to the dimension he wants, he uses a maul (a sort of oversized hammer), a chisel (a metal bar whose cutting edge is angled), a drill, a gradine (a kind of chisel with a toothed cutting edge), files and burnishers.

Hard materials most often employed are wood, stone and ivory.

Being in relatively good supply, wood is therefore inexpensive. Of the immense variety of woods, sculptors usually prefer fine-grained species, such as the walnut used by Flemish artisans in the Middle Ages to produce monumental altarpieces of fantastically detailed relief. Wood may be left in its natural state or else polychromed or gilded by applying gold foil over a coating of wood filler.

Stone poses more difficult problems, as quarries must be found and the material extracted from them. Marble, which is in reality a fine-grained limestone, has for aeons been favoured by sculptors. Certain quarries have been famous since antiquity: the white marbles from Mount Pentelikon near Athens, those from Paros (a small island in the Cyclades) and the Carrara quarries in Italy. In France, exploitation of the marble quarries of the Pyrenees began only in the 17th century. When marble is unobtainable, soft white limestones are generally employed. In addition to working soft limestones, Egyptian sculptors did not hesitate to tackle challenging and hard-to-cut igneous rocks like green diorite, black basalt and pink granites.

Ivory is the name given to the teeth of certain mammals as well as to elephant and rhinoceros tusks; its relative scarcity tends to make it expensive. Because of its intrinsic original shape, ivory is generally used only for small pieces.

Working from a scale model. As early as the Hellenistic period (1st century B.C.), many sculptors abandoned the contemporary technique of cutting directly into the stone and instead began to work from scale models made of clay or terra-cotta.

Artists would first make a model and then delegate the stone cutter of his studio to reproduce it in the desired scale and in the chosen hard material. For large copies, the cutter would use the so-called three compass method (proportional compasses and a curved compass), while for smaller pieces a special apparatus was employed. Such methods have been standard practice since the Renaissance.

For ages sculpture in metal has been popular despite the difficulties involved in mining and smelting ores.

Antique craftsmen — whose works belonged more in the

The Coronation of the Virgin. Polychromed and gilded ivory, end of 13th century. The gentle expressions are typical of this period. Louvre, Paris. (Photo Boudot-Lamotte)

realm of goldsmithing than sculpture—mostly used gold and silver in the form of thin hammered sheets. Yet this limited method resulted in such treasures as the gold mask of Agamemnon in the National Museum in Athens and the famous mask of Tutankhamen in Cairo.

Bronze casting. Casting statues requires a technique which is fundamentally opposed to that of direct carving. For example, let us take the casting of bronze, a material that has produced masterpieces throughout the long history of sculpture.

Bronze is an alloy of copper and tin, sometimes with a small proportion of zinc or lead. Its composition may vary widely depending on the mineral resources available in any specific country or period.

There are several methods of casting bronze, the two best known being sand-casting and the lost-wax method. The latter

Descent from the Cross. Polychrome wood, 12th century. The treatment of draperies and the nobility of the figure are typical of Burgundian Romanesque sculpture. Louvre, Paris. (Photo Boudot-Lamotte)

dates from antiquity. An exact wax copy, complete in every detail, is made of the original work and coated with a fireproof material into which openings are made to allow the molten bronze to be poured in and to let the molten wax and gases escape: the former are known as casting holes, the latter as vents. As the molten bronze is poured into the fireproof shell, the wax melts and flows out, to be replaced by the bronze which thus adopts the form of the original figure. Subsequently all that is needed to get a perfect reproduction is to file and burnish the metal cast.

Flora. Faience bust from Rouen, 17th century. Many decorative faience busts depicting the seasons were made by Rouen potters. Rouen Museum of Decorative Arts. (Normandy Photo)

In the sand-casting method, the model is cut up into sections and a separate sand mould made for each part. The bronze is poured into these and, when cool, the parts are filed and burnished, then assembled with rivets.

Contemporary techniques. Contemporary sculptors fully exploit the marvellous variety of new materials now available, and in order to work them they have created equally new techniques. Hence saws, hacksaws, blowtorches and welding apparatus have been added to the sculptor's stock range of tools. Many artists have a preference for sheet aluminium, zinc and steel, and a few have even gone back to forged iron, a material heretofore only employed in producing utilitarian goods. Among the other modern materials that sculptors favour nowadays are the various plastics and plexiglas, which offer a satisfactory range of colour, transparency and flexibility.

The extreme complexity of contemporary sculpture stems not from the development or extension of traditional techniques but from putting their very existence and purpose to question. In fact, some modern techniques are so far re-

9

moved from traditional values as to fall beyond the range of accepted forms of sculpture.

Naturally, the technique employed by the artist depends upon his goal and on the material he has chosen, and this choice in turn may hinge on a whole series of economic and technical factors.

The choice. Ancient sculptors were limited in their selection of materials to local products because of inadequate transportation. Wood, though perishable, was popular since it could be found almost everywhere. Nevertheless, in some Middle Eastern countries, such as Assyria, stone was laboriously hauled down from nearby mountains. The Persians substituted brick for this relatively rare material, and glazed it to add permanence and colour to their monumental reliefs. In Greece and Italy, where marble quarries are readily found, sculptors soon abandoned wood and terra-cotta except for utilitarian objects.

Engraving by Bénard, showing one of the steps in casting Bouchardon's bronze equestrian statue of Louis XIV by the lost-wax method. Bibliothèque Nationale, Paris.

Because of the complicated and highly skilled techniques required for metal-working, gold, silver and bronze were rarely employed and only for commissions of special importance.

The discovery of kaolin deposits at Meissen (Saxony) in 1709 and at Saint-Yrieix (France) in 1769 led to the production of true porcelain in Europe, where for centuries Western artists had tried unsuccessfully to imitate Chinese ware. The result was a wave of porcelain sculpture—coloured and glazed in Germany (the works of Kandler in Meissen) or unglazed, fine-grained biscuit-ware (like that produced by Falconet in Sèvres).

Apollo of Piombino. Bronze, about 500 B.C. This masterpiece of Greek sculpture represents a young *kouros*. Louvre, Paris (Photo Giraudon)

Thanks to scientific and industrial progress, modern sculptors now have a dazzling array of materials to work with. Besides the traditional wood, stone and bronze, modern artists can and do utilize plastics, aluminium, finished manufactured goods and even industrial by-products and waste. Quite often they employ several techniques and a variety of different materials in the composition of a single opus.

Use of materials. Statues composed of one or more materials requiring widely varied techniques have been produced throughout sculpture's history. Some of these statues, though no longer extant, have kept their legendary fame. Perhaps the greatest of these was the chryselephantine (gold and ivory) likeness of Athena which once graced the Parthenon's interior.

Polychrome, or the use of coloured paints and glazes to enhance the form and realistic aspect of sculpture, also had its adherents. Egyptian, Roman and Japanese sculptors all used colours, and even the marvellous Greek reliefs, whose stark white simplicity is so much admired in museums today, originally were covered with the liveliest of tints.

On the other hand, sculptors working in porcelain or stoneware were far more restrained in their use of polychrome. In France, the sculptors of Rouen, and Joseph Fauchier of Marseilles (18th century), considered polychrome too easy and instead sought an effect comparable to that of stone relief.

Young girl smelling a lotus blossom. Limestone, Egyptian, Old Kingdom (5th dynasty). An example of "hollowed-out relief" from a Memphite mastaba. Louvre, Paris. (Photo Boudot-Lamotte)

reliefs

In reliefs, the carved portions jut out from the surface of the material, and depending on the extent to which they do so are known as low relief (bas-relief) or high relief. Such a distinction is purely theoretical, of course, since no one has ever decided the exact degree at which a low relief turns into a high relief. Consequently, we shall simply use the word relief for them both.

One of the peculiarities of Egyptian art is that reliefs were cut either into the background or out from it. A carved-in relief has an outline deeply cut into the stone, and the enclosed shape is gently modelled, thus creating a line of shadow around the subject. In dimly lit areas such as tombs, however, the subject usually stands out slightly and is enlivened with bright colours.

A sculptor chiselling a relief must face approximately the same problems as a painter trying to represent a three-dimensional subject on a flat or two-dimensional surface.

Like painters, sculptors of reliefs have adopted a whole series of conventions in representing the human figure or the different planes of a scene.

In a relief, the human figure does not obey the laws of

frontality but is almost invariably shown in profile. Such a representation, generally an intellectual reconstruction, may vary according to the civilization concerned. The Egyptian example is the most outstanding: the head is seen in profile but the eye is full face, the torso is full face and everything below the waist in profile. Thus the artist has picked the most typical integrants of a human being and shown each from its most recognizable angle.

Sometimes, a scene's different components are shown on a relief or painting as a series of registers or superimposed horizontal bands. Thus both Romanesque frescos and the tympani of Romanesque churches consist of superimposed registers, and in 15th century Florence both Donatello in his reliefs and Masaccio in his paintings used this form of perspective.

A relief's internal arrangement follows the same laws as those of a painting. Thus the composition in vertical, parallel lines of the *Panathenaean Procession* (see page 58) creates an impression of calm, in contrast to the violence of Scopas' reliefs, where crossed diagonals break the rhythm of the whole. Reliefs may be associated with natural sites such as cliffs, though they are more often used architecturally to decorate the exterior or interior of buildings. In Greek architecture, for instance, reliefs may run continuously around the building as a frieze (*Panathenaean Procession*) or they may be a set of sculpted slabs (metopes) separated by vertical elements called triglyphs. Relief was a flourishing art form during the Middle Ages, when the portals (tympani and lintels) and capitals of Romanesque and Gothic cathedrals were entirely covered with decorative or story-telling reliefs.

Athena and the Giants, by Scopas. Marble, late 4th century. A detail from the main altar at Pergamum. Berlin Museum. (Photo Boudot-Lamotte)

sculpture in the round

By definition, sculpture in the round means isolated pieces around which the viewer may move and which are truly three-dimensional.

As in the case of reliefs, any size and material may be employed. A Tanagra statuette only a few inches high is just as valid sculpture in the round as the Colossi of Memnon. As opposed to reliefs, however, sculpture in the round may occur independently of any architectural setting, though niches to hold statues are often incorporated in buildings. Isolated pieces may also make up an urban setting, as when they are placed in public squares or form an integral part of fountains, and they may be located in gardens. Another difference between the two art forms is that while reliefs may depict an episode or historical event, sculpture in the round must express life and movement by seizing the crucial instant in any given situation through the elimination of accessories and details.

The essential aim of sculpture in the round is the harmonious arrangement and balance of volumes in space, for, as Paul Valéry wrote,

"the work must be planned to satisfy the eye from an infinite number of possible angles, to each of which may correspond an equally infinite number of light sources. Every step the viewer takes, every hour of the day, each new light source applied, gives the sculpture a fresh appearance . . ."

For a long time—and this was true all over the world—sculpture in the round was bound by the laws of frontality, i.e., the body was treated completely symmetrically in relation to a middle axis.

The best example of this can be found in Greek art. Virtually all 6th century B.C. *kouroi* (sculptures of youths) adopt the same frozen attitude: "lifeless limbs, expressionless faces. Conceived in two dimensions, the statue faces the viewer, the figure's two halves reflecting each other in absolute symmetry on either side of an imaginary line" (P. Devambez).

During the course of the 5th century B.C., expression began to appear on the faces, volumes of the body began to fill out and the arms were separated from the trunk.

Polyclitus of Argos created a canon of proportions (in

A Bourgeois of Calais, by Auguste Rodin. Plaster, 1884–1886. One of the preliminary studies for the famous bronze group cast in 1886. Rodin Museum, Paris. (Photographic archives)

Tanagra statuette. Terra-cotta, late 4th century. Tanagra workshops in Boetia excelled in making such figurines. Louvre, Paris. (Photo Boudot-Lamotte)

which the head represented 1/7th of the body), and his dictum was scrupulously observed for centuries. He also invented a standard pose, the "arrested walk," in which the body weight rests on one leg, the other being slightly bent and to the rear; the torso is lightly tilted and the body relaxed.

As balance is one of the major problems to be solved in sculpture in the round, large-scale works showing figures in motion often need support. The masses of which a statue or group are composed must balance one another aesthetically and physically around an imaginary line passing through the work's centre of gravity. Both Bernini's *Apollo and Daphne* and Myron's *Discobolus*, or *Discus Thrower*, meet this criterion magnificently.

Artists not infrequently resort to various tricks to prop their statues: figures may lean against a tree trunk or hold onto an animal at their side. An analysis of the lines of force involved in Puget's *Milo of Crotone* (see page 188) provides a better understanding of its composition and the reasons behind the accessories used in this famous group.

Myron's *Discus Thrower* ranks as a triumph of instability and balance: the athlete seems to revolve about an invisible axis while light plays on the carefully distributed volumes of the body.

The conflict between the static and the dynamic, as exemplified by Myron's *Discus Thrower* and Polyclitus'

Doryphoros (see page 62), may be noted in all civilizations and in all periods of art. Thus in Japan, the impassive serenity of the 13th century figure Minamoto Yokitomo diametrically opposes the violence of the guardians of the Todaiji Temple in Nara, though both stem from the Kamakura period. A similar exaggerated contrast may be found in 17th and 18th century

Miroku-Bosatu. Wood, Nara period. The refined simplicity of the pose, contemplative expression and shrewd treatment of the material have justifiably made this statue a famous example of Japanese art. Koryuji, Kyoto. (Photo Kôzo-Ogawa)

Europe, where baroque and classical sculpture flourished side by side.

Nevertheless, the artist's refusal to portray motion does not necessarily deny life to a statue, as proved by Roman or 17th and 18th century portrait busts, where the subject's individuality and personality clearly shine through.

The Discobolus, or **Discus Thrower,** by Myron, about 450 B.C. Roman copy in marble of the lost original. Many replicas of the masterpiece still exist, each with slight variations. Vatican Museum, Rome. (Photo Anderson-Giraudon)

PATRONAGE AND COMMISSIONS

The group of statues on Easter Island, those on the Athenian Acropolis, the sanctuaries of Nara and the cathedral at Reims all have one point in common: their expression of man's faith and his desire to praise his Creator.

During the Middle Ages, cathedrals went up all over Europe and the faithful from every social level vied with each other to stock them with artistic treasures. Among these was the *Virgin and Child* presented to the basilica of Saint-Denis, near Paris, by Queen Jeanne d'Evreux in 1339. A parallel situation occurred in the Far East where the Shosoin in Nara was built during the 8th century to receive offerings made to the colossal Buddha of Nara.

Church patronage continued through the Renaissance and the Counter-Reformation. But toward the end of the 17th century, princes of the church began to commission more and more works for their own personal collections and far fewer for the religious edifices that they controlled. Only in the past few years has religious art finally freed itself of standardized shoddiness.

The renewed popularity of equestrian statues, an art form which had not been seen since antiquity, derived mainly from the policy of Italian cities to honour their victorious "condottieri" or "tyrants." One of the finest of such works is Verrocchio's *Colleone* in Venice. Subsequently, from the 16th century to the present day, city squares have been decorated with this kind of memorial statue commissioned by municipal bodies, heads of state or other civic leaders.

In some cases an art programme ordered by a king or his ministers has launched the development of a certain type of sculpture. Thus the work that Saint Louis had commissioned in 1263–1264— for Pierre de Montreuil to carve recumbent figures for the tombs of his ancestors— was continued by Saint Louis' descendants to make the basilica of Saint Denis a museum of royal funerary sculpture. Likewise, Louis XIV's construction of Versailles led to a blossoming of garden statuary.

Tomb of Pope Urban VIII, by Bernini. Bronze and polychrome marble. Typical of Italian funerary sculpture of the baroque period. Saint Peter's, Rome. (Photo Scala)

Reclining Figure, by Henry Moore. Bronze, 1960. An example of sculpture at the halfway point between figurative and abstract art. Museum of Modern Art, New York. (Photo Massin)

collections

Because of their prodigious sculpted decoration, such monuments as the Buddhist sanctuaries of Japan and China, the Khmer shrines of Angkor Vat, the Greek temples and the great Gothic cathedrals could be considered museums even though their original purpose was quite different.

Whereas collections of paintings were formed at an early date in history, sculpture collecting remains relatively rare and consists of only small pieces or a few large ones.

The role played by private and public collections and their owners is very important. "The history of art lovers is the consequence, the necessary result of artistic creation, for works are passed from one hand to another. Everyone knows that Michelangelo's *Slaves* are in the Louvre, but to show that they were handed down by the master to Roberto Strozzi, then to Francis I, to Anne de Montmorency, to her grandson, to Cardinal Richelieu, then to the Duke and Marshal de Richelieu before going into the Louvre testifies to the admiration that they have commanded over the centuries and confers on their owners still greater renown" (E. Bonnaffé).

During the Renaissance, the Medicis in Italy particularly valued their collection of bronzes, Grand Duke Francesco devoting a special room in Florence's Palazzo Vecchio to them. Between 1580 and 1584, a member of the Gonzaga family had a special gallery built to house his collection of antique statues and bas-reliefs, and Pope Julius II, one of the greatest of all art patrons, assembled the core of what was later to be the Vatican's Museum of Antiquities. Julius engaged the architect Bramante to build the Belvedere Palace and its court lined with niches for Greek and Roman works; here he installed the Laocoon sculpture group upon its purchase in 1506.

The vogue for sculpture held sway on into the 17th century. Cardinal Mazarin of France devoted the whole lower gallery of his palace to carved works. It held, according to an inventory drawn up on the cardinal's death in 1661, 546 pictures and 326 busts and statues, most of which were purchased by Louis XIV.

Nicolas Fouquet, Louis XIV's ill-starred finance minister

(1615–1680), appreciated contemporary sculpture to a degree that perhaps contributed to his downfall. To decorate his château of Vaux-le-Vicomte, he commissioned Claude Poussin to carve the series of terminals which now grace the gardens of Versailles, and he had Pierre Puget sculpt the *Gallic Hercules* now in the Louvre.

Such monarchs as Charles I of England, Louis XIV of France, Frederick II of Prussia and Catherine the Great of Russia were passionate collectors.

The ardour of sculpture lovers is well exemplified by Sir Charles Towneley, whose

The Gallery of Antiquities, Palazzo Sabbioneta, near Mantua, 16th century. Both the architecture and decoration of this gallery were specifically designed to house a great collection of ancient sculpture. (Photo Alinari)

magnificent collection of antique statuary was acquired by the British Museum in 1805.

From the end of the 18th century onward, sculpture in museums became ever more important as museums replaced the private collections of antique statuary. Today the large majority of art patrons are inclined to buy both paintings and sculpture, neither exclusively.

The very earliest works of sculpture appeared in the Old World around 40,000 years B.C. during the Upper Paleolithic or Old Stone Age. Three major periods can be distinguished: the Aurignacian, Solutrean and Magdalenian. The tall, firm-jawed and athletic Cro-Magnons who lived during the first of these epochs stressed the female form in their primitive sculpture. In the third stage, Chancelade man saw animals as the principal subject matter. Between these two stretched the long Solutrean period, poor in sculpture though famous for its finely worked flint.

Aurignacian men tried to symbolize the continuity of the species in their sculpture. Mostly these were upright stones, roughly cut to form crude masks summarily indicated by eyebrows merging together and extended by a vertical ridge or groove for a nose. No neck separated head from body, but gashes in the stone indicated arms ending in a fringe of fingers whose number varied.

Ornament. Far more care was given to ornamental frills, such as belts or baldrics worn over

Cycladic idol. Paros marble. A primitive art form appeared in the Cyclades about 2,000 B.C. Simple figurines like this one were among man's first attempts to portray himself. Louvre, Paris. (Photo Boudot Lamotte)

23

the shoulder or around the neck. Relegating human features to second rank, sculptors concentrated on decorative details. The statue of Saint Sernin (Rodez Museum) wears a belt with two bosses brought out in relief; another at Puech-Réal wears a belt as shown by an indentation circling the waist, while the statue at Ponsthorny has a belt securely held in place by a rectangular buckle with a hollowed-out centre.

Female head, found at Brassempouy. Carved ivory. National Antiquities Museum, Saint-Germain-en-Laye. (Photo Giraudon)

Sexual attributes. Often the sex of these standing stone statues is doubtful, and some have been changed to convert them from one sex to the other. In principle at least, a beaded collar indicates a woman and a sharpened weapon a man. Nevertheless, there are male figures with cavities cut around their breasts to transform them into women. An exception is the charming female bust from Brassempouy, Landes department, France, a prognathous mask whose hair is bound in a sort of net.

On the other hand, other excavations have revealed indubitably female figures modelled in the round; these are the celebrated steatopygous (obese) "Venuses" of Willendorf in Austria, Lespugne in Périgord and Caussel in Dordogne, France, and Grimaldi in northern Italy. They have enormous bellies, pendulous breasts, small round heads and short thick thighs. The same general type has been found elsewhere in France and in Poland, Egypt, Thrace, Crete and Greece; the Aurignacian universe was a large one inspired by the same concepts. These statues were symbols rather than the representation of any particular woman.

Magdalenian art

Finally, steatopygous women vanished, the first differing type being the female statue found at Laugerie-Basse, France. Magdalenian sculptors, true artists, keenly observed nature and especially animals, as can be seen from the clay bison of Tuc d'Audoubert and the stretched-neck Lourdes horse whose hairy coat is carefully indicated by patient cross-hatchings. Magdalenian weapons show the technical development of these civilized men. In the beginning, they simply carved javelin heads from stag antlers. Later they cut saw-toothed notches on one side to eventually become barbs; the same technique was then applied to both edges to make it a true harpoon.

The Copper Age. Between the Paleolithic and Neolithic came the Mesolithic or Middle Stone Age which flourished so splendidly in the Dordogne region of France. The vigorous carved relief of a horse at Mas d'Azil eloquently testifies as to the march of progress. By this time, adventurous men of the Mediterranean had sailed out into the Atlantic in search of the Tin Islands, now known as Great Britain. Thus the Copper Age, typified by Cretan and Greek pre-Mycenean products, now gave way to the Bronze Age.

The Bronze Age. From Homeric Troy to the Baltic, bronze sword pommels and jewellery appeared as well as such figurines as the remarkable warrior bearing

Baetyl, or standing stone statue, from Saint-Sernin. Copper Age. At the same time that pure copper was first smelted, men tried to represent themselves in stone —here in granite. At the top of the stone are signs indicating features; below are grooves for arms and legs. It is a male figure wearing a strap belt from which a weapon dangles. (Photo Giraudon)

onto their scales. Four hundred years later, at a time when Romans still used hemp to moor their ships, Caesar in turn became fascinated by the fierce Bretons' anchor chains. Iron and bronze were worked simultaneously during the entire Hallstatt phase. A votive bronze chariot found at Strettweg in Styria is surmounted by a giant female figure holding a basin; she is escorted by mounted men and foot soldiers.

two shields found at Teti in Sardinia, and equally interesting objects excavated in Scandinavia.

While bronze remained popular, a new metal, iron, began to be worked across southern Europe from Hungary to Spain, especially in Burgundy, France, and at Hallstatt, Austria. Naturally enough, iron was first used for weapons; the Gallic chief Brennus amazed the defeated Romans by throwing his iron sword

La Tène civilization

The Iron Age. The Iron Age can be conveniently divided into two periods, the first, or Hallstatt phase, lasting roughly from 900 to 510 B.C. and the second ending in the Christian era's first century. The latter included the La Tène culture, so-called from a town on the shores of Lake Neuchâtel, one of the dynamic hubs of this civilization. The great works of Memphite Egypt, Minoan art and the Lion Gate of Mycenae belonged to the Bronze Age, while the war chariots and andirons, some of bronze or iron, others of clay and reflecting a Greco-Phoenician influence, exemplified the Iron Age. In the same tradition were some Gallic statues: a figure in oriental posture found at Roquepertuse in Provence and once thought to be a copy of the *Seated Scribe* (Louvre); a torso of an armoured warrior from Grézan near Nîmes; a naked kneeling javelin thrower found near Rome and now in the Berlin Museum; the *God of Bouray*, cast of thin bronze, and the stone bas-relief of the Gallic goddess *Epona* (Saint Germain Museum), who sits astride a mare following her foal.

In Ireland. Though ending on the continent toward the middle of the first century A.D., the La Tène culture continued to flourish in Celtic Ireland in an entirely original form. Human beings were hardly represented, and then in rudimentary form. Instead, extraordinarily convoluted linear patterns were carved in relief on baetyls, or sacred stones. The Celtic imagination invented a system of interlocking lines interspersed with fantastic monsters whose only rival in weirdness appeared in Viking art after the first Nordic invasions of about 775 A.D.

The God of Bouray. Sheet bronze, end of the La Tène period. Cast in several parts and crudely assembled, the figure shows the influence of the Roman occupation of Gaul. There seems to be no religious significance; the statue probably imitates the bust of a Roman emperor made by a Gallic craftsman. National Antiquities Museum, Saint-Germain-en-Laye. (Photo Giraudon)

THE EASTERN MEDITERRANEAN

The vast lands between the Red Sea and the Persian Gulf had been peopled by a stock of richly varied ethnic backgrounds: in the south, the Elamites who had their capital at Susa; in the west, the Sumerians who in all probability came from Anatolia or the Iranian Plateau. Excavations in lower Mesopotamia along the banks of the Euphrates have unearthed their main cities of Ur, Lagash and Uruk. These peoples had two things in common: a religion based on Ishtar and chthonian, or underworld, deities, and their own form of ideographic writing. North of Elam and Sumer were the Akkadians, Baal- and Marduk-worshipping Semites from Mesopotamia, who had their capital at Babylon. These originally nomadic tribes finally stopped their restless roaming, being peacefully transformed into farmers and craftsmen by the soil's fertility.

Gudea, King of Chaldea. Basalt, about 2,500 B.C. This extremely hard stone was carved with flint drills and then polished. The face is typically realistic. Louvre, Paris. (Photo Ségalat)

Kuduru of King Nilischipak, Assyrian, 4th century B.C. Basalt. The stele with its regularly arranged designs probably comes from a temple. The symbols and the astral signs which dominate the composition have a mystical significance, while the somewhat chimerical figures on the horizontal bands represent divinities. Sanctuaries visible on the horizontal bands add interest to this well-executed work. Louvre, Paris. (Photo Boudot-Lamotte)

The advance Neolithic civilization which appeared in Europe around 8,000 B.C. had developed some thousand years previously in such naturally blessed regions as Egypt and Chaldea. Five thousand years before Christ, copper was worked in Chaldea, mainly to make the weapons which ensured political strength.

Akkad and Sumer

The history of the primitive East was one of incessant clashes between city-states. With metal weapons, the Akkadians defeated their Sumerian enemies and kept them under heel for two millennia. Sumer subsequently recovered to regain its independence, but wealth became ever more concentrated in the temples, so that the people finally rebelled. Around 2,360 B.C., King Urukagine overthrew the priests, in what proved to be a futile liberation.

The founder of the city of Agade, Sargon I, subjected the mountainous regions of the north as far as the Black Sea, then went south to conquer Sumer and Elam. His successor, Naram Sin, man-

29

aged to maintain this empire. Yet some regions remained self-governing; the Sumerians of Ur and Lagash had been independent since 2,470 B.C. One of their sovereigns, Gudea, we have come to know very well through some finely worked and experienced sculpture. The Louvre in Paris displays several headless statues of this king, as well as separate heads depicting him. A very hard basalt is the material employed. Forceful broad modelling was achieved by patient abrasion, cutting tools being utilized only on the eyebrows, eyes and on the marvellous undulations of the heavy royal headdress. About thirty other representations of Gudea have been found. The king is shown either in prayer or as the builder of the temple, holding such architectural attributes as compass, ruler and square on his knees. Features indicate that Gudea was of Indo-European origin, as is the Louvre's noteworthy wavy-haired female bust with its little cap and clothes ornamented by inset lace. Eyebrows are delineated by a deep groove whose shadows produce the same effect as relief. This piece is Sumerian and dates back to the third millennium B.C.

Statue of Ebih-il, steward of the Temple of Ishtar in Mari, 3rd millenium B.C. Alabastar. Typical Sumerian art of the protodynastic period, this figure of soft stone wears a short sheepskin tunic and its eyes are painted on with tar. Details of the beard and fleece accentuate the sobriety of the flesh areas. Louvre, Paris. (Photo Boudot-Lamotte)

Stele of the Code of Hammurabi, King of Akkad. Carved and engraved diorite, about 2,050 B.C. Above the long cuneiform text of the laws dictated by Hammurabi are the symbols of the god Marduk, who inspired the law-giving king. In addition to its great historical value, this work can be considered an excellent piece of sculpture for its balanced composition, ease of movement and refined modelling. Louvre, Paris. (Photo Giraudon)

Babylonia

The independence of Ur and Lagash was short-lived. About 2,265 B.C. they were invaded by the Elamites who swept on through Babylon and beyond Akkad to conquer the Assyrian capital of Nineveh. Later Babylon came under the sway of an Amorite dynasty, whose greatest ruler was Hammurabi (c. 17th Century B.C.) A brilliant administrator, Hammurabi organized irrigation and promulgated a just code of laws. The Louvre owns a copy of this precious text engraved on a diorite stele (c. 1575 B.C.) in the cuneiform characters which replaced the primitive ideographic script. Babylon became the capital of this empire and remained so even under foreign dynasties: the mountain-dwelling Cassites from Zagros, who ruled from 1,761 to 1,178 B.C., and then the Semitic Armenians from the Iranian plateau.

Of all these peoples, only the Chaldeans and Assyrians, although of disparate race and abilities, left behind sculptured monuments of unchallenged artistic quality, surpassing technically and in spiritual content the craft objects used in everyday living. For all their ferocious reputation and historic arrogance, the Assyrians had a high aesthetic sense.

Assyria

Decorators at heart, the Assyrians bequeathed unforgettable images of the human face, almost exclusively in bas-relief. They heavily emphasized detail and accessories, such as the fastidiously braided hair and beards of gods and kings, the ornamentation of tiaras and the decoration of tunics—all carved with such precision that it is believed that these ornaments were the badges of power. By contrast, the sculptors used broad planes to define the naked flesh of faces, arms and legs in such a way as to accentuate the values of the composition. Muscles were delineated by sharp, clean lines.

Incidentally, the Assyrians never ceased to point up their subjects' social status by the most obvious means. Kingly figures all wear beards, their expressions invariably impassive; servants are clean-shaven, dull and unimaginative. In some bas-reliefs of warfare, enemy faces are not treated cursorily as before, but with a hint of pity that

Gilgamesh, bas-relief, Assyrian. Limestone. Though the head faces the viewer for a change, the sculptor has obeyed the laws of frontality by showing the legs in profile. Nonetheless, the forms are faithfully rendered and the hair and beard exceptionally well executed. The lion that the hero is strangling is also reasonably accurate. Yet the picayune detail seems to rob this work of its monumental quality, and only its dimensions make it colossal. Louvre, Paris.

Human-headed bull, Assyrian, about 2,500 B.C. Steatite. Half-human, half-animal forms were worshipped in Assyria as in the rest of the Middle East; in this case the human head is treated as realistically as the bull's body. Regular curls on the hide of the bull add a monumental note to this statue.

shows Assyrian art could be compassionate. Tricks or perspective were quite unknown. Like Sumerian Chaldea, figures are all on the same plane, one beside the other, never facing the viewer. Even the massive, tiara-wearing winged bulls with human heads who guarded the palace gates remained subject to the imperatives of bas-relief.

Animal art. Assyrian artistic talent attained its true fulfillment in the treatment of animals. The British Museum owns a group of superb bas-reliefs showing kinsmen Sennecharib and Assurbanipal both on horseback and in their chariots. These master-pieces come from Assyrian palaces at Khorsabad and at Kuyunjik, Nineveh, as does the Louvre's much lauded bas-relief portraying Assurbanipal standing in a canopied war chariot. The features and motion of both human and animal models are rendered with extraordinary finesse.

The Onager Hunt pictures the sudden panic of the herd. Some, pierced by arrows, roll about in agony while others have turned to fight off the dogs, and a few gallop off in terror. There is a similar fascinating bas-relief depicting a *Wild Goat Hunt;* still another shows the royal pack of hounds, enor-

Wounded Lioness, bas-relief, from Assurbanipal's palace, Assyrian, about 680 B.C. The same precision was used by the Assyrians in treating the muscle structure of both animals and humans. Eliminating all superfluous detail, they concentrated on the accurate rendition of masses in motion. British Museum, London.

mous mastiffs trained to bring down lions; and perhaps it is the lion hunt itself which best epitomizes Assyrian sculpture. An unusually memorable version is of a wounded lioness, dragging her paralyzed hindquarters yet still turning to bay defiance at her tormentors.

Chronologically the bas-reliefs from Nimrud are oldest. The conventional realism of Assurnasirpal sacrificing to the gods well typifies this period. Then there are the ones of Khorsabad with their more studied modelling, followed by those of Kujunjik which mark the apogee of Assyrian sculpture just before the fall of the empire. One of the striking aspects of this art is the total absence of females. The seated queen figure in the bas-relief of Assurbanipal's feast is a rare exception to this rule, for Assyrian art deals mainly with a warrior society.

Monsters. The Assyrians' profound knowledge of animal anatomy led to the creation of a whole range of weird and strange monsters. Besides the winged bulls with human heads, there is a winged god with eagle head, as well as a host of other bas-reliefs exhibiting this odd bimorphism. They include a winged horse of Nineveh, the sphinxes from Xerxes' palace at Persepolis and the griffons of Sennecharib's palace. The Chaldean-Assyrian east also summoned up the chimeras which appear nearly everywhere in ancient art.

Scenes from a military camp, bas-relief from Assurbanipal's palace in Nineveh, 7th century B.C. (Photo Boudot-Lamotte)

Stele of Naram Sin, king of Assyria and conqueror of Akkad, about 2,950 B.C. Louvre, Paris. (Photo Giraudon)

the Medes

North of Assyria lived the bloodthirsty and barbaric Medes whose leader Cyaxares in the year 606 B.C. attacked Nineveh, razed the city and split the remains of the empire with the Akkadians. Later he annexed Persia, giving his allies the kingdom of Judah. Yet the sudden change from primitive life to luxury proved too much for the Medes, who, once weakened, were no match for the Persians. Virtually nothing remains of Median art.

the Persians

Cyrus, the "King of Kings" (558–524 B.C.), and his successors extended their sway over all Asia Minor, first conquering Lydia under Croesus (580–524 B.C.), then Chaldea and finally Mesopotamia. Darius (521–481 B.C.) pushed on as far as the Indus. Liberal-minded, receptive to new ideas, he administered his immense empire without in any way trying to unify it, and for two centuries Achemenid princes ruled over this disparate universe.

The Persian civilization of this time left behind some splendid works of art, including the huge enamelled brick bas-reliefs of the *Archers* and the *Immortals*. Directly inspired by Assyrian art, these vast compositions possess a rhythmical architectural quality which was not without its influence on the Hellenistic East. They reflect the Assyrian concern for minute descriptive detail contrasting with broad sculptural planes.

Zoomorphic capital from the Royal Palace at Persepolis, Persian, 4th century B.C. Stylization confers a monumentality on these forms which otherwise might have been only colossal. Louvre, Paris. (Photo Ségalat)

the Hittites

We have but the most elementary knowledge of the Hittites. Still, we know they had a highly developed civilization. They were the first to raise horses, and 2,500 years ago—in their capital of Khattusas—they built palaces and houses with terraced gardens. Around 2160 B.C. the Hittites became powerful enough to threaten the strong pharaohs of Egypt. But Ramses III (1202–1171 B.C.) took his revenge in 1195 and the Hittite empire crumbled. They left behind a few sculptured pieces, all rather primitive, that drew inspiration from Assyria and Egypt.

the Phoenicians

The Semitic Phoenicians who established a beachhead on a narrow strip of the Palestinian coast were essentially sailors and tradesmen; their capital was the seaport of Tyre. Artistically unoriginal, they first based their sculpture on Mycenaean models, then on Hellenistic or Roman works. Even the art of their distant colonies like Carthage provided little that was new.

Alexander the Great's conquests between 354 and his

Baal of the Thunderbolt, from Ras Shamra, early 16th century B.C. Limestone. A fine example of formalism and frontality which, despite crude modelling, shows the trend toward ornamental stylization. Louvre, Paris. (Photo Boudot-Lamotte)

premature death in 323 B.C. opened the Hellenistic Age, and henceforth all Near Eastern art was to be strongly marked by the impact of Greek civilization. Antioch on the Orontes River, Dura-Europus and Pergamum became the major centres of this new culture (see page 68).

Serpent King stele
from Abydos, 1st
dynasty. Limestone.
Of the forms of the
falcon and serpent
and the architecture
they dominated, Old
Kingdom sculptors
retained only
volumes obtained
by slightly
hollowing out the
background. As in
the earlier style,
emphasis was
placed on types
rather than
individuals.
Louvre, Paris.
(Photo Ségalat)

EGYPT

It was some 5,000 years ago that the full-blown art of sculpture appeared in Egypt and created masterpiece after masterpiece. This sudden perfection presupposes a long apprenticeship, yet the total lack of examples from the preceding period leaves the origins of this art shrouded in mystery. Still, the earliest sculptures show a certain affinity with Magdalenian works—for example, in the expression of volumes and movement, and the inclusion of formal symbolical motifs as opposed to mere accessory details. Though we are, unfortunately, unaware of the reciprocal influences exerted by various peoples on each other at this time, certain similarities can be detected which could hardly be called coincidental. Subsequent discoveries have shown that quite apart from any aesthetic considerations, a religious principle inspired this sculpture, and nothing prevents us from attributing this same mystical purpose to proto-historic statues.

The Egyptians were not trying for portraiture but for a true representation of the personage that would instruct his *Ka*, the double who accompanied him through life and then, upon his physical death, took up residence in the image so as to assure immortality. Thus, in order for the *Ka* to recognize it, the image had to faithfully reproduce the person's features as well as his ritual or professional attributes. For this very reason, realism became the fundamental rule of Egyptian sculpture.

On being crowned monarch, a pharaoh's first concern was for his *Ka*, to ensure its survival in the tomb which was a replica of his palace. The earliest mastabas, or tombs, contained statues quite separate from the sarcophagi.

Later kings erected pyramids. Eighty of these still exist, the most famous being the one of Cheops, which dates back over 4,500 years and took 20 years to construct. According to Herodotus, over 100,000 workers were employed in its construction, and from the scenes found showing the transport of statues and building stones, the ancient historian's estimate seems well justified.

Accompanying the statue of the king are others, less finely carved but with equal regard for realism, of his servants, guards and craftsmen. His whole background lives again in these statues, whose execution was the more painstaking the higher the subject's social rank. Yet the Cairo Museum's famed statuette of the baker's wife and helper coating an amphora, or jar, with pitch, already foreshadows the broad, open style of the Louvre's *Seated Scribe*. While the stele of the falcon Horus in Cairo seems somewhat dry because of the resistance of the hard schist to the tool, the replica now in the Louvre attests to a sure mastery of both technique and aesthetic values, which aimed at essentials and nothing more.

Sheik-El-Beled, a village headman, 4th dynasty. Wood. Old Kingdom sculptors reproduced the subject's features at the same time that they idealized a type. Cairo Museum. (Photo Boudot-Lamotte)

Statue of Chephren, 4th dynasty. Diorite. Seated in a hieratical position, this statue is distinguished by the broadness of its modelling which is simultaneously realistic and typical. Louvre, Paris. (Photo Boudot-Lamotte)

Memphis

The first two dynasties established their capital at Tanis in upper Egypt; from this period stems the Louvre's Horus. Whether this was the product of a superior school in some Tanite town or simply that of a single genius is unknown. Works of this period

are of uneven merit, but on the whole indicate an attempt to express form through a contrast of planes rather than through the juxtaposition of detail.

Around 3,100 B.C., the seat of empire was transferred to Memphis in Lower Egypt, where it stood as capital from the 3rd to the 11th dynasty. This was perhaps the golden age of Egyptian sculpture, with such treasures as the diorite bust of Chephren, the polychrome figurine of Princess Nefrit, the beautiful wooden statue of Sheik-El-

Seated Scribe, 5th dynasty. Painted limestone. The modelling magnetically draws the viewer's eye to the face and torso. Excessive detail employed on the legs distracts from its interest. Louvre, Paris. (Photo Ségalat)

Beled (all in Cairo), and of course the Louvre's fabled *Seated Scribe,* whose eyes are animated by a silver nail. Here is remarkable individuality of features and a sincerely fresh approach untainted by any formalism. The bas-reliefs so popular at this time show the same pointed concern for the main

Offering Bearer, 12th dynasty. Painted limestone. Lofty monumental style is here beginning to generate into realism as stress is laid on individual details. Louvre, Paris. (Photo Ségalat)

motif. A light, cut groove separates the figures from the background, creating just the required amount of shadow. Egyptian artists continued using this process, though later they deepened the composition's line to convey the impression of still greater relief.

These artists stayed remarkably true to the professional techniques and traditions they had inherited. For centuries, standing royal figures remained attached to walls, a throwback to a time that had not learned to calculate the stresses on free-standing figures. Less exalted persons were represented with complete freedom, however, since ceremony did not concern them. From the very start of this period, Egyptian sculpture adopted the two paths it was to follow until the final decline—royal studios turning out statues of the pharaohs in a style which soon became a pat formula, and private studios seeking in general a picturesque style. Nevertheless, royal artists did not remain unaffected by their independent colleagues, and some of their solemn figures began to depart from a ritually hieratical posture. For instance, the *Ranofir* of Cairo Museum is walking, as is the Louvre's *Samonasrit* and the *Mikerinos*, who is framed by the goddess Hathor and another female companion.

Starting in the 4th dynasty, Memphite statuary showed a tendency to more idealization, though without sacrificing resemblance. Yet it was at this same time that factories began to mass-produce the figures of boatmen, brewers and archers which needed only to have a face sketched on in order to accompany their illustrious patron to the tomb. Stone cutters then simply carved the name onto these near replicas. At this point, the priests decided that it was not the statue itself but rather the name on it which contained a mystical virtue and which perpetuated the personality of the deceased. One result of this belief was that henceforth the pharaohs began to put their own names on the statues of others.

techniques

Nevertheless, sculptors continued to refer to the grandiose canons of the past, and the laws of frontality seen in the bas-reliefs still strongly influenced even their free-standing figures. In the bas-reliefs themselves, heads are seen in profile, the body full face, legs again in profile and always with the left leg forward. Whatever the sculptor's talent, this was a matter of pure practicality, originally justified by ignorance but substituting, as it continued, academicism for the objective study of nature. Still, there was a sort of system to it, and in covering surfaces with figures subjected to a form of triangulation, Egyptian

Men bringing tribute, Middle Empire bas-relief. Stone. Both humans and animals are truthfully represented with a freedom of movement which at times defies the laws of frontality. Louvre, Paris. (Archives photo)

sculptors seemed to have tried for a purely decorative effect. They carefully stylized components, thus preventing any naturalistic intrusion into arbitrary composition.

When, on the other hand, these same sculptors executed purely realistic groups, all stylization was excluded. Even the parade of offering bearers and the famous group of pikemen and archers in the Cairo Museum, though organized with a sharp sense of balanced masses, show a realism quite foreign to the decorative convention.

Starting with the Memphite period, two distinct techniques were employed in carving surfaces. Some works are cut directly in bas-relief in the stone, the subject being brought out from the bare ground and the light sliding across the modelling. Whatever anatomical mistakes may appear in such realistic compositions—for example, that of the cowherds in the tomb of Ptahhotep—the technique reveals real experience. More frequently, sculptors used the trick of carving a broad, deep groove around the main motif to give the effect of jutting out from a wall, though in fact the relief was quite shallow.

Thebes (2165–1800 B.C.)

Around 2,165 B.C. the Old Kingdom faded away rather than crashed, due to economic troubles combined with internal dissension. Then about 2,050 B.C. the energetic and warlike Sesostris dynasty established itself at Thebes in Upper Egypt. Political turmoil rarely has any repercussions in the arts, however, the latter being determined by the general cultural level of the times. Sculptors continued the realistic study of the individual that had insensibly crept into religious formalism, and even the official studios began to inject some life into the effigies of notables they were called on to sculpt. Unyielding hieraticism gave way—models were allowed a human gesture such as simply holding an object in their hands, and postures varied.

While the Old Kingdom had idealized its figures to create an impression of serene majesty, Theban sculpture seemed to stress realistic expression. Its pharaohs remained gods but were no longer idols. The *Tuthmosis III* in the Cairo Museum, cut from fine schist, is a portrait that is particularly cleverly modelled, as

slight modulations in lighting illuminate the planes, depending on the position of the viewer. Other examples of 12th dynasty work are the polychrome wood *Offering Bearer* of the Louvre and the *Head of an Old Man*, also of wood, now at Eton School, England. This remarkable example of the great Theban tradition is reminiscent of Cairo's Sheik-El-Beled in its simplicity, though the attempt to portray individual character shows the difference in approach of the two periods.

In the first Theban period, standard formalism was applied to official works, but under the influence of an increasingly free civilization, artistic virtuosity began to replace the august impersonality of the past. The *Pharaoh Horus* in the Cairo Museum is seen walking and relaxed, the sculptor's technique able and smooth.

secrets of style

The authors of these works seem to have deliberately rejected the rules to which classical sculptors had ad-

45

hered. Egypt had established a canon of proportions for sculpting life-size figures: the projection was ruled into eighteen squares, of which the top two covered the head, the next ten the neck and body as far as the knees, and the last six the legs, which invariably were long. Thus a rigid academicism became established. Nevertheless, this school produced a few outstanding personalities who escaped such backward-looking conformity, and the first Theban school had its quota of authentic masterpieces. Among them is the *Fighting Sesostris* in Istanbul (which Champollion held to be the acme of Egyptian bas-reliefs).

Tel el Amarna

Lower Egypt's occupation at this time by the Semitic Hyksos doubtless did much to stimulate the people of northern Egypt. The horse-raising Hyksos owed their dominance to new arms, including armour with bronze scales. They did not seat their leaders on the pharaonic throne but limited themselves to collecting taxes. Thus the succession of Egyptian dynasties continued uninterrupted, though in fact controlling but a small part of the country.

The last reigns of the 18th dynasty were darkened by civil war and foreign invasion. Yet the sculpture studios continued their work, after a trend which seemed to put extra emphasis on realistic detail. This troubled time produced the curious statue of the heretic pharaoh Amenhotep (Amenophis) IV, or Ikhnaton, which with its long vertical dominants was probably meant to be seen from below. This pharaoh moved the capital to Tel El Amarna, between Thebes and Memphis, thus reawakening the local sculpture studios whose output, though routine in execution, had a spontaneity and life missing from that of the official studios. The sculptors of El Amarna worked from nature, and the roughly chiseled statue of an anonymous personage now in the Berlin Museum so closely resembles the king that it is probably a life sketch.

The artistic flowering of this period can also be seen in the glittering gold funerary statue of Ikhnaton's successor Tutankhamen. In his brief reign the boy king managed to re-establish the old cult and dig the rock-cut tomb which held such astounding archaeological treasures.

Mask of Tutankhamen, New Kingdom. Solid gold. This pharaoh's effigy was found in his rock-cut tomb. Its tiara was decorated with a serpent, symbolizing knowledge. Cairo Museum. (Photo Giraudon)

Colossal statue of Amenhotep (Amenophis) IV, or **Ikhnaton,** New Kingdom. Stone. Cairo Museum. (Photo Boudot-Lamotte)

Amenhotep (Amenophis) III started the great funerary temple in Thebes, whose only remains are the two badly damaged but colossal figures, now known as the Memnons, guarding its entrance. One of his predecessors, Tuthmosis, felt that he could better assure his *Ka's* safety by abandoning the pyramid formula and instead cutting a shaft deep into the rock for his tomb. Colossal statues now guard the access to the Valley of Kings where these monarchs were henceforth buried.

47

Queen Nefertiti. Painted stone, 1,360 B.C. Theban sculptors of the New Kingdom individualized their subjects without, however, softening their style. Facial features are presented in detail, with eyelids and lip outlines lightly accentuated. Berlin Museum. (Photo Brückmann)

Head of the colossal statue of Sesostris, 18th dynasty. Diorite. In spite of damage, this statue retains the severe monumental quality of Middle Empire sculpture. Only the essential planes are brought out in the modelling and, seen at a distance, these reproduce the features. Louvre, Paris. (Photo Ségalat)

Ramses II

Pharaohs of the 19th dynasty, Seti I (1,326–1,300 B.C.) and Ramses II (1,300–1,234 B.C.), had to fight off the powerful Hittites who, having overrun Cappadocia and Phrygia, now threatened Palestine. Ramses eventually beat them at Kadesh, but even after twenty years of constant warfare he still had to share Syria with the invaders. He then started on the immense projects to which he owes his fame— the great temples of Karnak and Luxor, and the Ramesseum at Qurna (Thebes), dedicated to his glory. Also he commissioned the wonderful colossi of Abu Simbel which today may be seen in their original and glorious mountain setting.

The sculptors' virtuosity then became predominant, as can be seen from such characteristic works as the *Queen Taia* (Cairo Museum), the *Lady Naia* (Louvre), both carved in wood with consummate artistry, and such animal works as the statue of the divine cow Hathor now housed in the Cairo Museum. Hathor was executed with cunning; her nostrils (apparently worked with a toothed instrument like a file) seem to quiver with life and energy.

Lady Naia, New Kingdom. Wood. This young lady, wearing a light, close-fitting garment, has also a ceremonial wig reproduced in minute detail. Louvre, Paris. (Photo Giraudon)

the Saitic period

Events rather like those which had brought the Old Kingdom to its end now marked the history of Egypt between 1,085 and 663 B.C.—a lean period so far as sculpture is concerned. The royal shops continued to copy old works without in any way modifying their style through any direct reference to nature. Of the rare works showing any personality at all, we might cite that of the Sannafi couple in the Cairo Museum. Next to them in the same museum is a female figure with a large wig, her figure draped in a light fabric which allows all the delicate modelling of her body to show through. No less beautiful is the head of Queen Tiyi, or the canopic jar of Amenhotep IV with its wig and embossed collar.

Belonging to the same period is the small bronze of *Queen Karomama* in the Louvre. Despite the movement of her arms, outstretched to hold an offering, the sculptor could not bring himself to abandon the laws of frontality which governed the positioning of the legs. Still, the execution shows great skill, as exemplified by her body seen under the thin gown, the latter's lifelike folds and the designs

Queen Karomama, statuette. Bronze inlaid with gold and silver, 22nd dynasty. Posed with left leg slightly forward according to ancient custom, the standing queen wears a fine gown and a ceremonial wig. Virtuosity had become the hallmark of late Egyptian sculpture. Louvre, Paris. (Photo Giraudon)

on the bodice in damascened gold and silver. This technique, which involved hammering strips of precious metals into shallow grooves cut into the bronze, was also employed for the large falcon-headed statue of the god Horus, also in the Louvre.

Harassed by incursions of Ethiopians, then Assyrians, the Egyptians moved their capital to Bubastis in the Delta, thence to Saïs. There, under the last kings of the 26th dynasty, Egypt recovered its independence for a century until overrun by the Persians. During this time the old religion regained its authority, and sculptors paid increased attention to realistic detail. The British Museum now displays a relief of the pharaoh Psammeticus I (651–611 B.C.) which illustrates this: no slavish regard for aesthetics mars the brutal verisimilitude of his profile. The head of the Theban governor Mantimake, now in Cairo, also ranks as a forceful and expressive sample of the last truly Egyptian statuary.

Saitic art aimed at demonstrating its virtuosity. It showed a predilection for such intractable materials as basalt, diorite and marble, which were polished without

Horus consecrating a pharaoh, Saitic period. Bronze. The falcon god pours holy water over a figure which is now missing. Louvre, Paris. (Photo Ségalat)

51

impairing their basic structural nature. The style itself was of cut-and-dried practicality, figures being carved according to a strict formula. The Cairo Museum displays many examples of how the procedure worked—there are bas-reliefs in rough form, others carried to completion, and statues whose heads are mere blocks awaiting a client. Yet though the bodies themselves are banal in the extreme because of this mass production, the heads are most carefully executed. Funereal statues no longer represent an idealized young version of the defunct but a close rendering of his appearance, warts and all, at the time of death. The *Ka* was supposed to find in the statue an accurate reproduction of the living man.

In 342 B.C. the last Egyptian dynasty died away when the country became a Persian colony. Only a decade later Alexander the Great drove out the usurpers, founded Alexandria, and proclaimed himself the successor to the native rulers. When his empire was split at his death, Egypt fell to one of his generals, Ptolemy, who established his own Greek dynasty. The Hellenistic influence which blended with the other foreign elements can be seen mainly in architecture (as in the temple of Phylae), but it also affected sculpture, of which the most outstanding example is the bas-relief of *Antaeus and Isis* in the Cairo Museum. Its only virtue lies in its hybrid nature. Cultural traditions remained intact, however, and even in Ptolemaic Egypt, funerary statues continued to be made.

Torso of Isis, goddess of childbirth, Saitic period. Diorite. Here she wears a tunic whose pleats show a realism quite novel in Egyptian art. Louvre, Paris. (Photo Ségalat)

GREECE

The history of Greek sculpture starts with the rough-hewn wooden figurines, the Xoana, dating from several thousand years B.C., and continues down to the dawn of our own era. Once it assumed a definite shape, three styles evolved: the Ionian on the coast of Asia Minor, the Dorian in the Peloponnesus, and the Attic on the shore of the Saronic Gulf. A world-famous pre-Hellenic work is the Lion Gate of Mycenae on whose lintel are two rampant lions separated by a short tapered column. Rudimentary in style but still marked by an attempt at realism, it is thought to have been erected in the 12th century B.C. At this same time, artists in the Troad and Cyprus were modelling primitive figures from clay. Local tombs have given up many clay figures which show the artist's endeavour to express his view of concrete reality, as well as the influence of a more highly evolved East: Chaldea, Egypt and above all Minoan Crete.

Around the start of the current century, American archaeologists at Gournia unearthed a "Minoan Pompeii" which flourished between 1,700 and 1,500 B.C. Statues found there reveal considerable talent. The Knossos Museum contains many vases with walls decorated in relief, rhytons, and terra-cotta figurines of priestesses in scalloped dresses wearing tiaras. From Crete came also the model of a small temple in which the goddess takes a ritual bath, observed by two male figures on the roof. Similar terra-cotta works have been found in Mycenae. Like the rest of Neolithic Europe, Greece sent forth countless migrations carrying civilizing influences in all directions.

Early Greece elaborated its own forms, particularly in such island centres as Paros, Naxos and Chios. One of the very first masterpieces of Greek sculpture, the *Apollo of Thera* (Athens Museum) was produced in Naxos. Cut from a single slab of marble, it appears full face, arms at sides and feet parallel in respect for the laws of frontality. This archaic type of Apollo is not specifically Dorian in origin. According to Pliny the Elder, the island of Chios could claim some seniority in working marble.

the geometric style

The island of Samos concentrated on bronze. Originally the metal was hammered over a wooden form and the various parts then assembled "by means of nails," according to Pausanias. By about 700 B.C., however, the Samians had learned to cast bronze in a mould; Peloponnesian artists soon followed suit. The *Warrior* from Karditza in northern Greece, whose Dipylon shield seems to form two wings behind, shows to what extent techniques had progressed. Soon the lost-wax method was discovered for casting large works.

Dorian invasions obliterated these original forms to replace them with the "geometric" style in drawing. Flat and barely modelled, the statues of this period, like the *Hera* of Olympia, are closely related to architecture. Only toward the end of the 6th century B.C. did a reborn Greece produce works which, though still hampered by archaic formalism, at last reveal a completely new way of observing nature.

Ritualistic factors obviously dictated the way temple servants would be represented.

The statues of the ten Branchidae, or priests of the Temple of Didymean Apollo in Miletus (British Museum), are seated on stone blocks in the same posture assigned them by Chaldean and Egyptian sculptors—arms down at sides, hands (palms up) on knees. The *Apollo of Piombino* (Louvre), however, reveals a new freedom. An oriental influence can be seen in the bizarre figure of the Gorgon holding its offspring—the winged horse Pegasus—under its arm. Also oriental is the Greek adaptation of the Egyptian sphinx into a bird-like female monster.

Greece could thank the East for the rapid development of sculptural techniques. From points and abrasives, sculptors soon graduated to chisels which, working material on an angle, created planes over which light could play. Greece also acquired the knack of making statues stand independently, without accessory supports, and tried to breathe life and movement into them. Greek artists developed a method of using colours to accentuate relief and shadows in their sculptures, highlighting projections with lighter tones and darkening hollows with a mixture of red and black.

Attic sculpture

Spared the Dorian invasions, Athens continued to use woodworking idioms in its archaic sculpture. Carved of volcanic rock, the oldest reliefs in the Acropolis Museum—*Heracles Fighting the Hydra* and *The Triton*—seem to have been cut from wood. As for the so-called "Berlin Goddess" found at Keratea, the thick rigid folds of her *peplos* appear to be sawn from a tree. She is typical of the early 6th century B.C. Soon, Athenian sculptors were to drape their young girls in thin materials with undulating folds—like the famous *Aloof One* in Athens. The Louvre has a fine specimen of young

Bas-relief from the Treasury of Siphnos in Delphi, archaic period. Marble. The sculptor has used a clever combination of curved planes to avoid lack of expression in the opposed masses. Louvre, Paris. (Photo Boudot-Lamotte)

athletes, or *Kouroi*, in the *Rampin Horseman* from the Acropolis. Names of artists now begin to appear: Antenor, author of the beautiful *Athena Triumphant* and a *Titan* in the Acropolis Museum, and Archermos of Chios, sculptor of the *Flying Victory*. There was Pythagoras, too, who was the first to seek an expression of reality outside the traditional hieraticism. These artists anticipated Myron and Scopas by a full century.

The series of Persian invasions which devastated Greece between 499 and 465 B.C. left behind irreparable ruins; Greece had to rebuild from the ground up. However, much had been learned in the meantime. Now temples were built and decorated with reliefs using a proven technique. No longer was sculpture designed as a simple ornament for the building but as a coherent whole linking the structure's dominant verticals and horizontals. Arranged according to the theme being treated, each group of figures drew the eye while still remaining subordinate to the whole.

The Aloof One. Bust of a woman from the Athenian Acropolis, about 490 B.C. As the archaic period drew to a close, sculptors freed themselves from the bonds of convention and instead studied nature. The primitive Core thus became a living person. Acropolis Museum, Athens. (Photo Boudot-Lamotte)

The Rampin Horseman. Head of an archaic statue. Marble, 6th century B.C. Careful carving of hair and beard is typical of early formalism, as are the bulging eyes and the smile with its accents on the lips. It was just such formalism that the sculptor of "The Aloof One" (above) avoided. Louvre, Paris. (Photo Giraudon)

themes

Generally speaking, the themes handled were the assemblies of the gods, heroic feats, or mythological battles; the central figure, placed in the axis of the triangular pediment, determined their arrangement. Thus the pediment of the Temple of Zeus at Olympia portrays the battle between the Lapithae and the Centaurs. Apollo appears amidst all the violence and with a single commanding gesture brings peace. Awed expressions on the faces reflect his authority. The lovely Deidamia fending off the assault of a centaur with her arm has a solemn grace imitated throughout 5th century Greece. Anything foreign to the monumental, the timeless and the ideal was rigorously excluded. To the artist, a battle was a combination of forms on a wall, arranged so that the contrast of highlights and shadows produced the desired effect. In Greek sculpture the effect is obtained not by juxtaposition of details but by the interplay of volume over which light can dance. Figures can overlap and cover portions of one another, and the outline of the masses suffices to create a form of perspective.

Deidameia, relief from Olympia, about 480 B.C. Marble. The cowering figure of Pirithous' wife, arm lifted in self-protection against the assault of a centaur, is an archetype of Greek monumental sculpture; faces remain inexpressive and body motion is reduced to essential volumes. Olympia Museum. (Photo Alinari)

movement

At this time sculpture also sought to create the impression of movement, once and for all casting off the law of frontality. Figures are no longer static but caught at a moment when they change from one state to another, part of the body belonging to a prior phase and another part to the present. Movement is not seen as a posture but as a change of posture, and it is this subtle difference which the masters of the 5th century brought out.

More care was lavished on drapery. During the 5th century, female fashion abandoned the thinly pleated tunic, or *chiton*, worn by the *Aloof One*, in favour of the heavier, sleeveless *peplos* which stopped at the waist and was extended by a skirt. The drapery of these garments made possible an infinite variety of treatments either in the form of grooves, as in the tunics of the caryatids on the Erechtheum, or to emphasize the volume and form of the body beneath, as in the veil of the Lapith being carried off by a Centaur on a Parthenon metope. The procession of Ergastines in the Panathenaean frieze combines both effects.

Panathenaean Procession, detail, from the cella of the Parthenon, carved by Phidias' studio between 442 and 438 B.C. Marble. The vertical rhythm is accentuated by the regular arm movements. Louvre, Paris. (Photo Giraudon)

independent statues

Though sculpture became beautifully adapted to architecture during the 5th century, independent pieces also existed which retained all the monumentality of statues seen full face. Starting about 480 B.C., the bronze casters were able to produce such works as the *Charioteer* (Delphi) in his ritual *xystis* with its graceful full-length pleats.

Myron, who was probably born about 490 B.C. in Boetia, turned out a series of masterworks between 450 and 420 B.C. which "put more emphasis on body than soul," according to Pliny the Elder. Of Myron's *Discobolus*, Lucian so aptly wrote: "He leans over to throw the discus, turning his head toward the hand that holds it, and bending his knee slightly so as to rise again once the discus is on its way." The charming

Charioteer. Bronze, about 473 B.C. This figure formed part of a group commemorating the victory of Gelon and his driver. The official winner is shown in the conventional nudity of heroes, while the charioteer wears his racing garment, or *xystis*, which reveals the strength of his arms only through the folds of the sleeves. Delphi Museum. (Photo Alinari)

Athena Threatening Marsyas (Frankfurt Museum) is one of the first attempts at making a face expressive, and the *Wounded Niobid* in Rome, an admirable nude, seems to retain her classical serenity even as she collapses. Here again Myron showed his originality; before his time, all female figures were clad and even Aphrodite was veiled. Previous sculptors had only considered nudes in the gymnasium where the young athletes were trained.

Polyclitus, born in Argos about 470 B.C., followed in Myron's footsteps and apparently worked until the very end of the 5th century. He was responsible for the *Doryphoros,* of which the original bronze has disappeared, though a marble copy stands in the Naples Museum. His study of motion is no less penetrating than that of

---

Athena, part of a group of which the other figure, Marsyas, is now missing. Marble copy of an original bronze by Myron of the mid-5th century B.C. The goddess is seen forbidding Marsyas to pick up the lute she has thrown to the ground. For the first time, the Boeotian master has given a face some expression and emphasized it by a slight twist. Frankfurt Museum. (Photo J. P. Vieil)

Athena Lemnia, marble copy of a bronze original by Phidias of about 450 B.C. The body of that statue, in its *peplos* tied by a simple cord, is in Dresden's Albertinum, while the head is in the Bologna Museum. This masterpiece is the culmination of Athenian classicism. (Photo Alinari)

Wounded Niobid, from Sallust's gardens. Marble, about 450 B.C. In trying to pull out Apollo's arrow, the girl has let her *peplos* fall, revealing her breast and thigh. The admirable rendering of motion is enough to express her pain, as her face remains immobile. National Museum, Rome. (Photo Alinari)

his elder contemporary: the young athlete calmly strides forward carrying a heavy combat spear, the weight of his body shifting to his right leg as the left leaves the ground. Polyclitus' contemporaries considered his work so perfect that they summarized it in a phrase—"the rule." A master theoretician as well as craftsman, Polyclitus plotted his statues according to set proportions in which the head accounted for one seventh of the total height. The *Diadumenos* (Athens Museum), again a marble reproduction of a lost bronze, copies the movement

61

of the *Doryphoros* but with an extra distinguishing grace. Polyclitus saw the work of Phidias on an Athens visit in 430, learned a great deal and took the lesson to heart. But he lacked the poetic imagination as well as the fertile inventiveness of Phidias.

Phidias was born in Athens about 490, being entrusted in 437 by Pericles with the works which Polyclitus saw being completed. Around 438 his studio carved the *Panathenaean Procession*, at the same time that the great chryselephantine statue of *Athena Parthenos* was being dedicated in the newly built temple. Every Greek author of the time praised the beauty of the Parthenon works, be they of marble or ivory and gold. Of all the sculpture that they described, precious little remains: a few heads in Athens' Acropolis Museum, parts of the Panathenaean frieze in the British Museum, and the *Athena Lemnia*. The head of this statue, executed by Phidias around 450 B.C., is now in Bologna and its body is in the Dresden Albertinum. Rarely has sculpture ever provided such modelling for the interplay of light. This work represents the acme in the long history of Greek sculpture.

The Doryphoros, marble copy of a bronze original by Polyclitus of about 445 B.C. In the relaxed stride of the confident athlete, this male nude ranks as a superlative example of the Dorian genius. Naples Museum. (Photo Brogi)

4th century

Sculpture veered off in a new direction after this golden age. Four names lent distinction to the new style, the first being Leochares, author of the *Apollo Belvedere*, *Artemis the Huntress* and *Ganymede and the Eagle* (Vatican). The others were Scopas, Praxiteles and Lysippus.

Aphrodite of Cnidus, marble copy of a marble original by Praxiteles of the mid-4th century B.C. A prime innovator, Praxiteles was the first Greek sculptor to show the female body completely unveiled. Vatican Museum. (Photo Alinari-Giraudon)

Venus de Milo (Aphrodite of Melos). Original Parian marble, 4th century B.C. The unknown creator of this work was the first to reveal the female torso. Louvre, Paris. (Photo Bulloz)

Maenad, copy of an original marble by Scopas of the 4th century B.C. The damaged fragment of this work leaves unanswered the question of its facial expression, but the body's violent motion suggests the savage ecstasy of this priestess of Dionysus. Albertinum, Dresden.

Praxiteles, like Phidias an Athenian, was born about 390 B.C. and reached his peak around 360. He inherited the technical ability of his illustrious compatriot, but where Phidias sought solemnity and depth, Praxiteles looked for grace. One of his favourite subjects was a young man leaning against a tree trunk, as can be verified by the *Apollo Sauroctonus,* of which the Louvre has a marble copy, and the *Hermes Carrying the Infant Dionysus* (Olympia), which is actually an original. Naturally enough, a sensitive sculptor of male nudes could not completely ignore the female figure. As early as the beginning of the 4th century, the unknown author of the *Venus de Milo* (Aphrodite of Melos) had shown the female goddess half-draped. Praxiteles let the last veil fall, and his *Aphrodite of Cnidus* opened a new field.

Scopas of Paros, who flourished about 420 B.C., had preceded Praxiteles in this development, though no example has come down to us. We have only the testimony of many contemporary Greek authors who speak of the passionate character of his work. A small marble copy in the Dresden Albertinum of a maenad orgiastically tearing apart a kid may be justifiably attributed to Scopas. The violence of the maenad's twisting body and the energy of the style can be found nowhere else in Greek sculpture. It is an expression of pure mystical passion.

Lysippus, born in Sicyon about 375 B.C., claimed that he was not a disciple of Polyclitus but of that master's *Doryphoros.* Apparently he was self-taught, and after a careful study of nature invented a new style in which movement predominated. An analysis of his extant works confirms this, as in the typical *Apoxyomenos Athlete* (Vatican) whose outstretched arms displace all the muscles of the torso.

Lysippus can be credited with changing the canon of proportions of the human body since his figures are not seven but eight times the length of the head. Nevertheless, he did not seem to apply this system too rigorously. His main aim was to produce the sense of form in motion which the viewer could appreciate from any angle. Lysippus was also the first to make the most of live models, rejecting "the square structures of former times," as Pliny put it.

toward realism

Later the great Roman naturalist observed that "After Lysippus, art stopped," though he had plenty of opportunity to view works done after the master of Sicyon had departed. Around 300 B.C. an unknown sculptor (probably Doidalses) executed the *Crouching Aphrodite,* of which many copies exist, including one in the Louvre and another in the Vatican Museum.

About the same time a statue was commissioned to celebrate the victory of the Greek fleet over the pharaoh Ptolemy in 306, and its style leads us to believe the author was influenced by Scopas; this was the fabled *Winged Victory* found at Samothrace in 1863 and now one of the glories of the Louvre. This Nike is not in flight nor on the point of landing, like the badly mutilated version by Paianios in the Olympia Museum. Instead, the Nike of Samothrace is leading the Greek fleet into combat as she stands on the prow of the lead ship, wings outstretched and *peplos* crushed against her body by the wind and salt spray. Both statue and pedestal seem to be moving relentlessly forward (see page 4).

later masterpieces

Pliny was too quick to condemn the new realistic style, for it too could claim its masterpieces. Typical of the "literary" style is *Menelaus Recovering Patroclus' Body*, dating from about 300 B.C. and reconstructed in Dresden's Albertinum. The hero's desperate attempt to drag off his friend's inert body, away from the insults and threats of the enemy, are conveyed with utter naturalism.

Equally accurate rendering was employed half a century later by the unknown sculptor of the *Wounded Gaul*,

now in Rome's Capitoline Museum. Utilizing the same treatment employed for the *Menelaus*, the nameless author of this work executed it to commemorate the victory of Attalus I, King of Pergamum (241–197 B.C.), over the invading barbarians. Still supporting the corpse of his wife, the Gaul is seen stabbing himself in a frenzy of grief.

Both of these are magnificent works which reveal the talent of the sculptor rather than any profound emotional inspiration. They attract mostly because of their technical virtuosity and strong expression: poetry and spiritual content are lacking despite the high drama. A typical example of the trend can be found in the famous *Laocoon* group. Detail is perfect, muscles and expressions are treated with consummate workmanship. Yet the wild gestures of the group spoil the composition, and the overall effect is one of bombast instead of feeling, theatricality instead of emotion.

Battle of the Gods and Giants, from the main altar of the temple in Pergamum, 2nd century B.C. Marble. An example of how monumental sculpture degenerated into mannered virtuosity. Berlin Museum. (Photo Giraudon)

Child with a Goose. Marble copy of a bronze original by Boethus of the 2nd century B.C. Here was the first Greek sculpture to truthfully portray children. Sculpture Museum, Munich. (Photo Boudot-Lamotte)

Rare indeed were any works harking back to the early concepts. Such a one, however, was *Athena Seizing Alcyone By the Hair* (main altar, Pergamum). Still rarer were realistic studies of children, such as the *Child with a Goose* now in Munich's Sculpture Museum. By Boethus of Chalcedon, this was probably the earliest prototype of "genre" statues.

Crouching Aphrodite. Marble, 3rd century B.C. With its highly individualized face, this work was executed in a spirit far from that of the classic tradition. Vatican Museum. (Photo Alinari-Giraudon)

the Hellenistic period

Alexander the Great's conquests opened the Hellenistic period and spread Greek culture from Egypt to Asia Minor. Pergamum became one of the capitals of the Hellenistic world, while Dura-Europos and Antioch founded flourishing schools of art. Throughout this area, art was henceforth to be based on Greek models, as can be seen from two Pergamum works, the celebrated *Head* of *Alexander the Great* and the *Kneeling Venus Doing Her Hair,* whose form may be a bit lush but whose movements are certainly graceful.

Simultaneously, an oriental influence began to be felt in Greek sculpture, and the first result was an attempt at technical virtuosity. Sculptors tended to give too much importance to detail, distracting the viewer and destroying the work's unity. The *Battle of the Gods and Giants* (from the main altar at Pergamum), of which fragments are now in the Berlin Museum, strikingly

Woman carrying child, Hellenistic period, from Palmyra. British Museum, London. (Photo Boudot-Lamotte)

illustrates this artistic deviation: Carved during the reign of Eumenius II (197–159 B.C.) and originally 390 feet long by 7½ feet high, this gigantic frieze has drill-cut foliage with the same sculptural value as its human features.

Alexandria, founded by the Macedonian conqueror on the Nile Delta, soon became the scene of important sculptural activity. Using a new technique in bronze casting, one of its studios produced the famous *Apollo* or *Colossus of Rhodes*, a 100-foot statue considered one of the marvels of the ancient world and which was only brought down by an earthquake some fifty years later. The Alexandrian school was also responsible for popularizing reliefs composed much like paintings, and this "pictorial" style quickly spread to other centres of Hellenistic art.

Antioch, on the other hand, produced a figure of *Tyche*, the patroness of good luck, of which a copy still exists. A formal classicism marks the Hellenistic influence in this case, and this can also be said of the carved decoration on Alexander's sarcophagus which was discovered at Sidon in Phoenicia.

terra-cotta figurines

At this time, too, the Greeks created a series of works which, though not of such noble materials as marble or bronze, nonetheless revealed major sculptural trends. These were the terra-cottas which first appeared at Tanagra in Boeotia and later were imitated throughout Greece and Asia Minor, particularly at Myrina. Like full-scale sculpture, these figurines had evolved slowly over the centuries. First came the rough figures found in Neolithic tombs, followed by ever finer work from the Troad, Mycenae and Crete. Originally clay was modelled by hand, but after the technique of moulding clay developed around 600 B.C. a whole new art idiom grew up which, while popular, was at the same time extremely elegant. These figurines drew their inspiration from larger contemporary works but never imitated them. Only the essential principle, that of rendering through volume instead of through the juxtaposition of details, was kept. The familiar subjects treated are not only of great importance in revealing the development of customs and clothing but also the development of the plastic arts.

ROME

In prehistoric times, two distinct peoples came to occupy Italy: the native Latins who made their home in Rome's surrounding swamps, and the Etruscans who settled in present day Tuscany.

the Etruscans

These latter seem to have arrived in Italy about the 11th century B.C., bringing with them a civilization strongly marked by oriental influence. By the 7th century B.C., archaic ceramic ware from Greece had been imported; soon the Etruscans developed their own technique. Though they knew how to carve stone, they primarily used wood for their architecture. The Tarquin dynasty which began to rule in 616 B.C. built Rome's fabled sewer, the cloaca maxima, using the mortarless masonry method of the Greeks; it exists intact today. That the Etruscans could cast bronze is amply exemplified by the celebrated She Wolf nursing Romulus and Remus (Capitoline Museum) and the Child with Bird (Vatican).

Another Etruscan talent was in terra-cotta. The Lydian Tomb in the Louvre assumes the form of a couch on which the dead man and his wife half recline. We know little of the Etruscan religion, but the way the dead were individually represented, as in Egypt, leads us to believe that they too felt the necessity for a physical image that their spiritual double could inhabit after death.

Although Etruscan art reached its apogee in the 6th century B.C. with the Lydian tomb, a turning point had been reached back in the 8th century with the production of fine canopic jars meant to hold the ashes of the deceased. The 6th century saw the Greeks establish many trading posts and cities on the Italian mainland (Sybaris, Cumae, Locris, Paestum), as well as in Sicily (Agrigentum, Selinunte) after the arrival of Pythagoras. Lysippus also spent much time in Sicily.

The only Etruscan sculptor we know by name, Vulca, who carved the head of Hermes from the temple at Veii, was apparently a disciple of the Greeks. Yet he had two un-Grecian traits in his work: individuality of subjects and an intensity of

The bronze ram's head now in Palermo dates from the 3rd century B.C., it is true, but it still shows the same energetic treatment. Originally from Syracuse, it is a handsome creature carved with immense skill and craft. The artist has insisted on the animal's lascivious quality. Also very unlike the Greek outlook is the remarkable carved stone *Warrior's Head* of 530–520 B.C. found in Orvieto and now in Florence; and the bronze warrior from Brolio in the same museum, presumably cast about 600 B.C. Etruscan sculpture never shows the slightest intention of spiritualizing or transcending reality. On the contrary, reality seems to be the goal, and originally moulds were made of dead men's features so that bronze death masks could later be cast.

expression utterly foreign to classic Greek works. The Etruscan bronze *Chimera* in Florence's Archaeological Museum is still more revealing. Its monstrous appearance, accentuated by a goat's head implanted on its back and a serpent's head terminating its tail, conveys quite a different feeling from those fantastic creatures that the Greeks invented under their strongest oriental influences.

Sacrificial scene, bas-relief. Marble, 1st century B.C. The bull is a grand example of animal art, and here the sculptor has reproduced its supple form with rare economy. Louvre, Paris. (Photo Boudot-Lamotte)

This intense search for reality distinguishes Etruscan art from that which had preceded it, without much change from prehistoric times, in Sardinia and Lombardy, and which was centered around the town of Villanova from the 8th to the end of the 4th century B.C. The only remains of this Sardinian culture are grotesque figures of warriors with shapeless heads. In these short-coated figures a Mycenaean, Cretan or even oriental influence can be seen.

early Rome

Through courage, a new zest for hard work and a genius for organization, Rome progressively dominated Latium and the banks of the Tiber before going on to control its immediate neighbours. It then swallowed Etruria, from which it gleaned much instruction in the arts; and by the 3rd century B.C. had conquered Sicily and the rest of "Greater Greece." In doing so, Rome encountered a cultural heritage that could not be rivalled. Realizing this fact, Rome began collecting Greek originals, mainly of bronze, had them copied in marble and finally imported the artists themselves from

Greece. Native Roman sculptors seemed unable to develop without this inspiration, and even so the spirit was entirely different. Nevertheless, by the 3rd century B.C. Romans had developed their own formula, the foremost example of which is the bust of *Brutus the Elder* now in Rome's Capitoline Museum.

From this time on, two distinct tendencies grew side by side. First came the Hellenists who had faithful or free copies of Greek works made for themselves. Then there were the patrons who ordered works from Roman artists which more closely reflected the native genius. In any case, it is interesting to compare Roman copies with remaining Greek originals and to observe the different techniques employed.

Greek sculptors attacked the stone obliquely, creating planes on which light could rest. An examination of a Greek original by flashing a beam of light on its surface

The Emperor Augustus. Marble, 1st century B.C. The figure is seen wearing armour and holding back a full-length cloak. The frankness of the technique, and the use of contrasting planes, reliefs and hollows, shows strong Greek influence. Vatican Museum. (Photo Scala)

reveals a series of narrow facets which hold the light and over which it slides, depending on the angle of vision. The Roman procedure was something else. Artists attacked the material head on, and the result is a flattening which is only accentuated by polishing and which deprives the work of surface light even though the forms and volumes of the original may be exactly reproduced.

Detail of the frieze from the procession of the Ara Pacis. Marble, 1st century B.C. The flexible modelling, which distributes light to bring out the shapes of the draped bodies, is typically Greek in technique. Louvre, Paris. (Photo Giraudon)

realism

The realism which gives them their expressive power is the predominating feature of these works. On this point again it is worth remarking on the disparate character which exists between Greek and Roman art. In Greek sculpture the artist traced the composition on the block, outlining shadows and enclosed recesses which made the relief stand out. Romans worked in a quite dissimilar fashion—primacy was given facial features. Resemblance rather than character was sought, though the latter emerged anyway through

Husband and wife. Terra-cotta relief, 1st century B.C. A typical product of an art which valued accuracy above all in portraiture. Louvre, Paris. (Photo Boudot-Lamotte)

sheer truthfulness. Romans did not seek Goethe's "characteristic type" but rather the reality of the moment, and the bust of the first Brutus is in reality a portrait.

Centuries failed to change the essentially realistic and spiritually empty aspect of Roman art, which remained purely descriptive. Some six hun-

Bust of Seneca. Bronze, 1st century A.D. A representative Roman work in that the portrait's strength stems from the attention to detail. National Museum, Naples. (Photo Alinari-Giraudon)

Equestrian statue of Marcus Aurelius. Bronze, 2nd century A.D. The simple realism of this masterpiece in Rome's Piazza del Campidoglio is typically Roman, free of any Greek inclinations. (Photo Alinari-Giraudon)

dred years later, in the 3rd century A.D., an unknown sculptor carved the two busts known as the *Roman Couple* or *Cato and Portia* (Vatican), and he sought the exact same rendering, the same prosaic honesty. There is a scarcely noticeable relaxation in the treatment of drapery and hands. The bronze bust of *Seneca* now in the National Museum, Naples, falls somewhere between these two periods. The viewer's eyes instantly are drawn to the strands of hair and beard, and it is only later that one feels and appreciates the structural impact of the head, its sure modelling, and the character of the subject. This fine bust was executed in the 1st century A.D. From the same period comes the bust of the Empress Julia, wife of Titus (Capitoline Museum). The face and neck are cut into the marble with broad but delicate strokes, their purity unmarred by insistence on detail.

Similar in spirit and execution are the busts of Caracalla in Naples, Nero in Florence, Nerva in the Vatican and the fine statues of Agrippina in Naples and Augusta in the Louvre. During the 2nd century A.D., bronze casters produced the only Roman equestrian statue in existence, the magnificent *Marcus Aurelius* now in Rome's Piazza del Campidoglio. The horse prances in perfectly paced motion, his rider firmly seated in the saddle. Here again, Roman realism masterfully rendered the subject but was unable to transcend the mundane: it produced a wax-like effigy of a ruler on horseback. The Greeks would have made him the epitome of an emperor.

Bas-relief from the Arch of Titus, Rome, 81 A.D. The soldiers carting off loot are treated simply enough to create a monumental effect. (Photo Scala)

decorative sculpture

This fundamental discrepancy carries over just as strikingly in decorative sculpture, particularly in the triumphal arches which were one of Roman architecture's wonderful inventions. These were erected to celebrate the glorious events that they depicted, as for example the Arch of Titus built in 81 A.D. to commemorate the capture of Jerusalem eleven years previously. The bas-reliefs which cover it show the action of the siege and the soldiers returning afterwards with their booty. Highlights contrast sharply with deep shadows in the confused reliefs, and the story told must be deciphered word by word. There is no dominant figure on which the eye can thankfully concentrate.

The same is true of the Temple of Minerva built dur-

Bas-relief from Trajan's Column, Rome. Marble, 176 A.D. In contrast to the higher portions of the column, the lower parts are more carefully executed since they can be seen close up. (Photo Boudot-Lamotte)

of Trajan erected in 176 A.D. in memory of the Roman victory over the Dacians. Its extraordinary bas-relief spiralling up to a height of a hundred feet includes over 2,500 figures, and describes the battle which drove the barbarians away from the Empire's eastern confines. Legionnaires clamber about to operate siege machines; galloping horsemen bear down on groups of the terrified enemy; and foot soldiers fight hand-to-hand with their valiant adversaries. No detail is spared—and this in the long run becomes its main attraction. Yet it is precisely because of such evenness of interest that the column is looked upon more as a document than a monument. It tells of an important historical event but the light shimmering on this infinitely detailed relief makes the eye dart about without satisfying its need for a focal point.

Ornamental sculpture follows the same formal path. Dissatisfied with the Greek acanthus, Romans invented a composite capital with three rows of clustered leaves, and for the simple rosette they substituted the ornate ceiling roses which decorate the caissons of the Tabularium Museum.

ing Nerva's reign, of which a portion of the entablature and two columns still stand. Its decorative scheme remains visible despite the badly mutilated frieze; except for one or two bare parallel bands, everything is carved. Though the overall effect is opulent, monumentality is completely lacking. There is no decisiveness, and it appears as a blown-up version of some goldsmith's work.

Perhaps the most outstanding example of this undiscriminating realism can be seen on the marble column

decadence

Even the colossal statues of decadent Rome lacked a sense of monumentality: the enormous figure of Constantine, erected on the Capitol in the 4th century A.D., was conceived as an oversized figurine. The sculptor had no understanding of scale and failed to grasp that, seen from a distance, a huge form must be summarized in a few vital planes. In any case, this was perhaps the nadir of Roman sculpture.

Another horrid example may be seen in the red porphyry *Tetrarchs* now set into the facade of Saint Mark's in Venice. It shows four embracing figures representing the emperors who assumed joint responsibility over the Empire in 293 A.D. Diocletian kept Asia Minor for himself, allocating Italy to Maximian, the two Gauls to Constantine Chlorus, and Thrace to Galerius. These four figures, with identical features, dress, arms and movement, reveal the complete decadence of an art of which the bronze statue of Saint Peter, cast in the 5th century and preserved in Rome, is the culminating work. This figure is lifeless and without character. Yet in the 3rd century

Romans were still able to achieve elegance in casting the bronze *Doe* (Naples Museum), a beautiful and rare "animal portrait."

Head of the colossal statue of Constantine. Marble, 4th century A.D. During the decline, sculptors accentuated the features of their subjects without any sacrifice to style. Capitoline Museum, Rome. (Photo Anderson)

asia, pre-columbian
america, oceania, africa | 3

INDIA

The origins of Hindu art are obscure. This art first appeared some 250 years before Christ without having undergone the laborious evolution and the usual trials and errors found in the artistic past of other civilizations. To date, archaeology has been unable to solve this mystery, although one explanation is that primitive artists worked only in a material — wood — unfortunately susceptible to the ravages of time. Primitive Indians had neither architects nor sculptors, since the Vedic religion that they followed required no temples or clergy, and called rather for daily sacrifices to abstract deities. Equally undemanding was Brahmanism, which expanded rapidly about eight centuries before Christ. Its doctrine concerned mainly the sanctity of life and its continuity through the transmigration of souls.

Dancing Siva. Brahman art. Bronze, 8th century. The god of destruction, who is also lord of dance, is seen stamping a dwarf demon underfoot. Balanced forms are the result of symmetry. Musée Guimet, Paris. (Photo J. A. Lavaud)

Prince leaving the Kapilavastou palace, relief from the Sanchi stupa, 2nd century B.C. Typically Sanchi in style, this fragment presents a profusion of carved motifs without detracting from their legibility. (Photo Rapho)

Headless statue of the Serpent King, from Nagaraja. Hindu art. Red sandstone, 2nd century B.C. The powerful rendering of the face and the curve of the drapery accentuate the cleverly executed twist of the body. (Photo Boudot-Lamotte)

Brahmanism

During the 4th century B.C., however, a new Brahman theology made the distinction between two life principles: Brahma the male element, and Maya the female. Under Hinduism, this later evolved into the trinity of Brahma, the creator; Vishnu, the conserver, and Siva, the destroyer.

Such gods required temples and symbolic images. Consequently, India's sculptural creations between the 3rd century B.C. and the 6th century A.D. were inspired by Brahman ideas and governed by structural considerations. Stone pillars and architraves were assembled like wooden risers and cross-beams, carefully tenoned and mortised. Decoration also followed the traditions of carved woodwork, as can be seen from the balustrade medallion from Bharhut, one of the oldest Hindu monuments (Calcutta Museum).

Dating back to the 2nd century B.C., this piece typifies Indian sculpture in that no surface is left uncarved and that, while decorative elements proliferate, they all remain perfectly visible. It also amply demonstrates still another facet of Hindu art—the stylization resulting from the figures' anonymity. Concerned solely with illustrating an episode, sculptors superimposed different elements without any regard for perspective, trompe l'oeil effects, or even proportion.

Mystically inspired, Hindu art rejected individuality, and the stock figures represented are generally all young adults. When sculptors tried to give their work expression, they did so through mime and movement, openly and frankly: faces remained impersonal and impassive. Themes treated were solely religious.

Buddha

Buddha, who was to found a dynamic new religious philosophy, was born a prince of the powerful house of Sa-kya in the Benares region towards the end of the 7th century B.C. He proclaimed the equality of all living creatures and called for the abolition of caste. By 250 B.C. his disciples had converted southern India and the coast before carrying the word to Indonesia.

Nevertheless, by the start of the Christian era, Buddhism had changed and adopted some of the tenets of Brahman theology. The resulting schism, or mahayana, soon led to tantrism, which pushed to extremes the doctrine of the respect for life which forbade the killing of any living creature.

The formalism resulting from this compromise can be seen in Hindu art. Only at a relatively late date and as an exception did Indian sculptors descend from their mysterious heights to interpret human actions. The decorations of the Krishna caves show unusual realism in their representation of such mundane subjects as motherhood, musicians, cows at milking or the extraordinary *Descent of the Ganges*, in which enormous elephants tower over human figures.

Religion gave the stamp of mysticism to sculpture, which eventually resorted to violence and the colossal in an attempt to express the divine. Originally, a material representation of Buddha would have been considered a sacrilege, and therefore his godliness was shown symbolically: by the *triratna*, representing Buddha, his law and disciples, as on the Sanchi gate (1st century A.D.); by the *chiskra*, or wheel of the law, representing his teaching, or by the fig tree under which he received illumination.

human representation

Still later, Buddha was allowed to be portrayed in human form, a cultural revolution probably due to Greek influence. Greek-inspired Buddhist sculpture first appeared about 320 A.D. when Hellenized Scythian princes introduced Greek art and civilization to the northern part of the subcontinent, without, however, any permanent results. Characteristic of this sculpture are the Europeanized head, drapery similar to but heavier than their Hellenistic counterpart, and Buddha's pose. He is seated in the *adamantine* posture, his hands clasped idly together and his crossed legs hidden by the folds of his tunic, as seen in the statue in the British Museum.

By contrast, colossal Buddha statues of completely Hindu inspiration embellished many temple sanctuaries. Here four symbolic motions were shown: hands crossed over each other to show *meditation*, the left hand touching the fingers of the right to indicate *teaching*, the right hand raised in the "no fear" gesture, or the left hand open and releasing the right hand to signify *supreme illumination*. Invariably Buddha is seated, his right leg folded over the left, showing the sole of the foot in the so-called "subactive" pose.

The Sarnath Buddha. Stone, 6th century. Buddha is seen here in the teaching posture. Both the figure and the surrounding decorative elements bespeak an unorthodox Khmer influence. (Photo Boudot-Lamotte)

realism

The Gupta style. Later under Brahman influence, the god was more often shown standing, carved in semi-relief against a background, as in the still primitive 2nd century red granite statue carved by the sculptors of Mathura, now in the Musée Guimet, Paris. Under the Gupta dynasty in the 5th century, this same school of sculpture showed Buddha clad in a thin, finely pleated tunic, his head more freely treated and backed by an elaborately decorated halo. The Gupta style, deriving its name from the dynasty which ruled India during the 4th and 5th centuries A.D., did much to popularize Buddhism. Buddha statues were erected everywhere and, along with them, figures of those who had received illumination, or *Bodhisattvas*.

Brahman art. Humanizing the symbol of serenity brought Buddhist art closer to the Brahman, which concentrated on the weird, the bizarre and the exalted. Thus in the sculptured cave at Ellora, containing a striking relief in which the fantastic is mixed with violence, Vishnu in the form of a lion-headed man is seen fighting devils. The same group contains a dancing Siva, whose twisting body movements verge on decorative stylization. However, this distortion is a fairly realistic sculptural portrayal of the contortions involved in ritual dances whose object was transcendental transfiguration.

At the same time that sculptors of central India, with incredible patience, carved the mountain of granite at Ellora to decorate temples dedicated to Indra and Kailasa, other sculptors were at work in the southern part of the country. Here they produced equally elaborate works such as the marble horses and humans on the pillars of the Srirangam temple. Always, sculpture was a matter of virtuosity, though the traditional canons were adhered to lest a transgression should irritate the gods.

themes

As in its literature, Hindu visual arts leaned heavily on the erotic. Even Buddha himself never condemned carnal desire, barring it only when it troubled inner serenity and not in itself as forming part of the cosmic whole. Brahmanism, on the other hand, made sex an essential artistic theme symbolized by the phallus or *linga*. The act

Headless statue of Buddha, from Mathura, Gupta style. Red sandstone, 2nd century. Western inspiration is evident in the transparency of the thin garment. Its undulating hem recalls Byzantine traditions. Musée Guimet, Paris. (Photo Boudot-Lamotte)

of love is depicted in many art forms, and with considerable discretion at least until the 13th century, when a trend toward contortions became evident. The cult of Siva also became popular at this time. The god of evil is frequently shown, either dancing and waving his four arms or seated among his demons. The Musée Guimet in Paris has a remarkable bronze of the god dancing within a flame-fringed circle and stamping a dwarf demon under foot (see page 81).

decadence

The extinction of the Gupta dynasty had little immediate effect on the development of Hindu art, nor did Harsha's reconstitution of the old empire in the 7th century. After Harsha's death in 647, however, the country was divided into many principalities, each developing its own aesthetic depending upon the influences at play. Meanwhile, the Moslem tide had swept over the vast Indus plain. The primitive traditions were kept in southern India, and Hinduism seemed to withdraw into its own rich past. The literature of the period produced the *Puranas*, or Antiquities, a mine of informa-

Sacred dancer, relief from the temple of Kajuraho, 11th century. Returning to its old traditions, medieval India was nevertheless unable to rid itself of all Greek influence. (Photo Bergonneau)

tion on the early Vedic religion. But in the visual arts, and sculpture in particular, academic formalism became the rule. The violent motion of ancient works was carefully reproduced but the underlying inspiration had fled.

KHMER SCULPTURE

Civilization reached the peoples of southeast Asia—the Chams of modern Annam, the Khmers of Cambodia and the Thais of Thailand—only at a relatively late date, about the 6th century A.D. Living on the seashore, they influenced each other and were open to the lessons of more advanced civilizations. Khmer art, though it developed independently, owed much to Indian influence.

Successive empires that the Khmers created under the authority of their god-kings were centered at Sambor, Angkor Thom and Angkor Vat. Each ruler erected his own temple, or *Meru*, usually a step pyramid surmounted by a sanctuary dedicated to the god Siva, whose vital energy was symbolized by the *linga*. Heroes too were deified, and temples or statues celebrating their apotheosis abounded. The outcome of this religious outburst was a sculptural tradition alternating between Buddhist serenity and Brahman exaltation.

the Chams

The Chams of Southeast Asia were an aboriginal people of Polynesian origins. Only rare examples of their art survive, one being the Po Klaung Garai tower dating from the 13th and 14th centuries. Another, in Paris's Musée Guimet, is a fine 10th century bas-relief of exceptional style from Mison, near Tourane in central Vietnam. While the anatomical accuracy of the dancer represented is only approximate, this piece approaches great sculpture, thanks to the dancer's impassive features and the almost geometric form outlined by his moving limbs. Contrast between the two opposing styles of Cham culture can best be seen by comparing the above dancer with the 9th century seated statue of Siva in Zurich's Rietburg Museum. Here Siva wears the demoniacal grimace of an evil spirit.

the Khmers

There is a quite different situation in the case of Khmer. Its seesaw history, in which times of greatness alternate with periods of decadence, can be traced from the way old motifs suddenly revive and flourish.

Several distinct periods may be discerned, though they do not necessarily correspond with any political changes. During the first, which lasted from the 6th to 9th centuries A.D., the tendency in sculpture was toward realistic naturalism similar to that found during the Old Kingdom in Egypt. In the first half of the 10th century, realism gave way to conventional hieraticism. This was not a deviation but simply the sculptor's choice of what seemed the most important features.

Altogether dissimilar is a third period (second half of the 10th century), signalled by carvings on the Banteay Srei temple atop Mount Kurlasa. A relief of Siva is inscribed by two counter-curving arches on the pediment. Siva's foliage throne stands above horizontal bands on which differently scaled devilish figures dance in fiendish abandon.

The Musée Guimet in Paris houses another relief from this same temple. It shows the brothers Cunda and Upacunda, swords drawn, in a fight over an Apsaras (water nymph) whom they grasp by one arm. The figures' measured action, balanced composition, delicate modelling and naturalism foretell a new feeling in sculpture, represented by the same museum's Buddha, which came from Angkor Vat and must therefore be two centuries later.

Demons fighting, relief from the temple of Banteay Srei, 10th century. Chinese influence shows in the stylization of the demons, particularly those that are part of the main subject. (Photo Rapho)

Angkor

Here Buddha sits on the coils of the sacred cobra Naga, who spreads his great hood as if to shield the god with a canopy. Calm, impassive and serene, Buddha's features epitomize elegance. The feeling differs radically from that found in Hindu sculpture, for the subtle nature of Khmer art is entirely opposed in concept to Hindu hieraticism. The so-called Tara statue (Musée Guimet) provides a sterling example of this approach: the figure is no longer seated in any traditional pose but is kneeling, and his face wears the enigmatic "Angkor smile."

Above: **The so-called Tara statue.** Gilded bronze, 10th century. The facial expression is characteristic of this art. Musée Guimet, Paris. (Photo Boudot-Lamotte)

Left: **Apsarases,** bas-relief from the temple of Angkor, early 12th century. The hieratic figures of the dancers are less a natural presentation than a stylized decoration, accentuated by the limbs' angularity. (Photo Butler-Rapho)

Bayon

A like sensitivity appears toward the end of the 12th century in the sculpture of the Bayon, a temple in the Khmers' second capital of Angkor Thom, founded by King Jayavarman VII (r. 1181–1219). The giant mask of the Bodhisattva Lokecvara is probably a faithful portrait of this ruler. Under this monumental yet extremely human face lies a sumptuous bed of foliage, on which writhes the sacred cobra Naga, whose multiple heads rear at both ends. This too was a characteristic motif of Khmer art.

Another Khmer mythical beast is the lion Song, whose gaping, gap-toothed jaws betray Chinese influence, reflecting a lack of inventiveness in Khmer art in the realm of imaginary animals.

Khmer realism

Until the empire's collapse in the 13th century, Khmer art continued its sincere treatment of everyday reality. The most prosaic themes were used to decorate temples and shrines, though this banality in no way detracted from the delicacy of their large compositions.

A frieze in the temple of Angkor Vat shows three sacred tiara-wearing and egret-plumed Apsarases in the contortions of their extraordinary acrobatic dances. They are framed in elaborate foliage. By contrast, the reliefs of the Bayon temple in Angkor Thom depict the more popular theme of fishermen braving waves on a sea teeming with all forms of aquatic life, a subject undreamed of by the more hieratic Hindus.

King in triumph, bas-relief from the Bayon temple in Angkor Thom, late 12th century. A file of captives escorts the prince. The combination of realistic detail with decorative intent is revealed in the parallelism of the moving forms. (Photo J. M. Fontaine)

91

CHINA

Art appeared in Central Asia as far back as 2500 B.C., and it shows tremendous skill of execution even though the only artifacts which have come down to us consist of hand-shaped, wheel-finished pottery.

This art flourished during the Shang dynasty (c. 1523–1027 B.C.), whose capital later became a bronze casting centre; and indeed, throughout history China remained a leader in bronze. The various-shaped vases made by Chinese smiths were an important part of ancestor worship. Symbols of ritual sacrifice, and supposedly endowed with a mystical power of their own, they became the object of a strange form of veneration. Some marble sculpture dating back to the 14th century B.C. has been unearthed, but its quality of carving falls considerably short of the mastership achieved in bronze and ceramics.

In the 11th century B.C., the Shang dynasty was overthrown by the Chou people, but this palace revolution had little influence on artistic activity. From 771 B.C. on, feudal squabbles dominated the land until the beginning of the 2nd century B.C. In 202 B.C. the Han dynasty rose to power and managed to reconstruct the dismembered empire.

The Han period, which lasted until 220 A.D., was responsible for some admirable ceramic and bronze urns.

the Han dynasty

Of modest origin the first Han leader, Liu Pang, became a brilliant general and reformer of the imperial administration. He favoured Confucianism, which allowed deities to be represented only in symbolic form: a scaly, fire-breathing dragon became the imperial seal; a phoenix with a dragon body and pheasant head symbolizing immortality became the empress' emblem; the unicorn meant perfection, and the wide-mouthed wolverine protected man against evil spirits. A philosophy which thus opened up a universe conceivable to mankind naturally excluded any primitive abstractions. Art, which had been limited to combinations of linear forms, now turned to the study of nature.

Figurine of a horse. Painted terra-cotta, Han dynasty (202 B.C.–220 A.D.) This statuette belongs to the earliest period of Chinese ceramics. Despite primitive modelling the subject's character is well reflected. (Photo Manshichi Sakamoto)

A number of Han dynasty graves have yielded not only beautiful bronze and ceramic vases but clay objects of all kinds from ordinary daily life: chicken coops and barns, pig sties and even the model of a residential pagoda now in the Royal Ontario Museum, Toronto. The ornamental style of Han art is characterized by a lushness and interlacing of forms whose exquisite detail is its chief merit. Some funeral chambers were decorated with bas-reliefs in which the area around the subject was hollowed out, a technique reminiscent of pharaonic Egypt.

For a long time the quality of Chinese stone sculpture remained far below that of other art forms. Thus the stone horse trampling an enemy underfoot, dating from 117 B.C., is but a roughly executed sketch, while contemporary glazed earthenware figures of animals, such as squat Mongolian horses, have all the simplicity and strength of great sculpture.

the Six Dynasties

The Hans in their turn disappeared under a maelstrom of feudal dissension at the very time that the Huns and Protomongols invaded northern China. Protomongols were zealous Buddhists who carved religious images in bedrock, as can be seen from the cliff statues of Shansi (460–480

A.D.). They turned out many isolated figures which, though primitive in execution, are outstanding for their movement and natural expressions. Much of the Chinese aristocracy fled south from the invasion and between 221 and 589 the so-called Six Dynasties ruled from the imperial throne in the newly established capital of Nankin.

Soon contacts were established with northern China through Persia, which was then under Graeco-Buddhist influence. A new formalism consequently came into being, a sort of classicism exemplified by several interesting little pieces. The flavour of these terra-cotta statuettes is so Hellenistic that it seems hard to believe they are actually of Chinese origin. The stylized naturalism of the great gilded bronze Buddha of 477 (Metropolitan Museum, New York), and the way the tunic clings to the body, shows how beautifully these two artistic traditions can be combined.

The period's realistic approach may also be seen from the strong volumes and moulded drapery of a stone deified hero from the rock-cut temples of Shansi in northern China (Boston Museum of Fine Arts).

Head of Buddha. Stone, 4th century, Wei dynasty. National Museum, Tokyo.

the Tang dynasty

In 618 a new Chinese dynasty, the Tang, succeeded in re-uniting the empire of the south, but though its leaders remained in power until 907 they were unable to drive out all foreign influence. From this period come the charming clay figurines meant to accompany the dead into their next life. The Seattle Art Museum has a wonderful collection of these figurines, including actresses, horsemen, camels with drivers and fully equipped ox-carts.

Contemporary sculptors executed statues in the round following the example of Hindu and Sassanid masters in neighbouring countries. The old-time style with heavy drapery was abandoned in favour of sinuous, bare-torsoed figures wearing only light, pleated fabrics. But if the sculptor wished to treat a heroic theme, and depict a warrior or temple guard, the treatment altered drastically as he sought to impress the viewer.

In 755, the Tangs were shaken by a rebellion, and the weakened oligarchy tried to re-establish a tradition which could consolidate their strength. Rejecting Buddhism as a foreign import, they again turned to Confucian Taoism and the philosophy of Lao Tse (born 604 B.C.). There are many figures in China's sculpture heritage of this great thinker, who is depicted as an old man sitting astride a water buffalo.

Bodhisattva from Nara. Painted wood, 7th century. Chinese sculpture moved toward realism, maintaining a monumental simplicity by sacrificing superfluous detail. Metropolitan Museum, New York. (Photo Boudot-Lamotte)

the Sung dynasty and its successors

In 960 the Sungs seized power and managed to hold onto it until 1279. The founder of this dynasty was such an able administator that a long period of peace followed.

From this period, the Boston Museum of Fine Arts has a fine wooden statue of a Bodhisattva, transformed by now into the female deity Kuan Yin. She is shown seated in the classical posture of "royal disdain," with one foot on a footstool.

China was now fated to suffer a still more terrible onslaught, for in 1279 Genghis Khan's grandson, Kublai Khan (1215–1294), overran the country with his Mongol hordes, established the Yüan dynasty, and crushed the peasantry with intolerable burdens. Not until 1368 did a Chinese leader arise to expel the invaders. He was Chu Yüan-chang, who aroused the people against their oppressors and founded the Ming dynasty, which lasted until 1644. This period produced the marvellous "China white" porcelain statuettes in which the art of sculpture so beautifully joined that of the ceramics.

With the fall of the Mings, it was the Manchus, called in by a provincial governor, who succeeded in subjugating the entire country. However, it was only with the emperor Kang-hsi (1662–1722) that they became completely dominant. Once again, porcelain and bronze cast by the lost-wax method predominated, with monumental sculpture limited to a banal imitation of past glories.

Statuette of Kuan Yin, guardian of motherhood, gilded bronze, Sung dynasty. Museum of Eastern Art, Oxford, England. (Photo Giraudon)

JAPAN

Repeatedly invaded first by Mongols and then by Malays, the Japanese archipelago remained sunk in barbarism for centuries. The barren temples of the animist Shinto religion forbade any reproduction of its principal deity, the life-giving sun.

Korean origins

The first figurative art to reach Japan came in the form of Buddha figurines, imported by Korean monks during the first years of the 6th century A.D. These religious foreigners erected monasteries in the capital of Nara, where local artists tried to copy the imported models.

Korea at that time was divided into three kingdoms, none strong enough to ward off foreign invasions such as the Mongol onslaught of 1231. Only a few Korean works from these early times have survived. It is thought that the polychrome wood Bodhisattva, known as the *Kudura Kwannon* and now in Japan, may have been executed in Korea, though it could equally be a Japanese

Head of Buddha, Nara. Bronze, 7th century. Japanese artists adopted a chaste style in their treatment of Buddhist themes imported from India. (Photo Kōzō Ogawa)

copy of a Korean original, like the copy in the British Museum.

Nevertheless, we do know the creator of the Nara *Triad*, which shows Buddha in the "no fear" pose flanked by two acolytes. This gilt bronze statue was cast in 623 by Tori, a member of a Korean family which had emigrated to Japan in 532. The Seoul

97

Temple guardian, Nara. Wood. Japanese artists loved the grotesque. The temple guardian's expression is carefully calculated to inspire terror. (Photo Kōzō Ogawa)

materials

To escape the domination of the Buddhist clergy, the Japanese transferred their capital from Nara to Kyoto in 793. In the 8th century, they began to cast glorious bronzes such as the colossal Buddhas which may still be seen at Nara and Kamakura. Earlier bronzes were given a greenish-brown finish, but in the 7th century a beautiful black patina was developed.

Rarely did the Japanese use stone in their sculpture, preferring bronze, polychrome wood and terra-cotta. Between the 6th and 9th centuries, the two traits which were to mark Japanese sculpture until modern times—Buddhist simplicity and exaggeration to the point of caricature—had become well entrenched.

Museum has a fine 7th century gilt bronze statue of the Buddha in which he assumes a position quite foreign to the Hindu canon. Seated with his legs folded, he reflectively touches a finger to his chin. A wooden bust of Buddha in Kyoto seems to be a local copy of this work. From all appearances, it would seem that, at least during the early empire, Japanese sculptors faithfully imitated Korean prototypes.

Luckily, many works from this period still survive. They include, from the 7th century, the bronze Bodhisattva in Nara, done in the Tang style, and the painted terra-cotta *Gakko Bodhisattva*. Also of terra-cotta are the fearsome *Lukapala*, or guardians of the faith whose images accompanied the dead to their tombs and of which many fine examples may be found in Nara's Todaiji temple.

original characteristics

Subsequently Japanese sculpture freed itself of the aridity resulting from its graphic outlook, and precise outline was abandoned in favour of a study of volumes. In the 7th century lacquered wood statue of the *Bodhisattva Maitreya* in Kyoto, clearly cut planes give the impression of closely fitting sheets of metal. About 640, however, forms became both more flexible and richer, as can be seen from the seated figure of *Kwannon*, whose posture with the right leg crossed over the left seems to stem from a Korean prototype.

The original characteristics of Japanese sculpture—Buddhist idealism and an attempt at dramatic intensity —returned in the 8th century.

Starting in the 10th century, the Japanese pantheon was enriched by new arrivals. Besides the Buddha, the faithful worshipped Kwannon, goddess of charity, Yeso, the guide and protector of travellers, and then the gods of pleasure, beauty, and wealth. Naturally enough, Japanese artists portrayed such benevolent superbeings as friendly. Quite opposite was the ferocious aspect given to the evil

Meditating Bodhisattva, statuette, 9th century. Sure of his mastery, the sculptor here has abandoned canonical convention to demonstrate his talent. (Photo Giraudon)

spirit Fudo or to the god of war. A monastery in Nara has a magnificent statue of the latter featuring facial snarls and furious gestures.

the apogee

From the 12th century onward, the samurai sought to rebuild on the ruins of war, and two major artists emerged: Unkei (1142–1212) and his pupil Kaikei, both of whom aimed to reproduce the original masterpieces of the 8th century. Yet the polychrome statue of Vasubandhu shows an ease and naturalism of a new kind, and despite Unkei's efforts to carve wood into clean planes, his wonderful savage effigy of the King-guardian of Todaiji in Nara retains a flexibility lacked by artists of the earlier period. It was Unkei who fathered the highest expression of Japanese realism, a wood statue of the priest Monchakou now in Nara.

This period represents the acme of Japanese sculpture. During the 15th and 16th centuries two styles vied for honours: the school of Kano which concentrated on realism and that of Toso which revered academic elegance. Toso won out during the 17th century while Kano disciples held sway in the 18th.

No mask, one of several traditional types. Polychrome wood, 18th century. Musée Guimet, Paris. (Photo J. A. Lavaud)

masks

The masks used in Japanese theatre form part of that country's sculptural tradition. As early as the 8th century, actors used masks in performing mystery plays, and when the secular No theater emerged in 1370, the old papier-mâché and lacquer masks were given up in favour of painted wood ones.

Characters in this type of drama included Mambi, a naive young girl; Doji, a young man; Akoujo, a wicked old man, and the withered Yace Onna, a pathetic sunken-eyed crone with hollow cheeks.

Brazier, volcanic stone, Olmec, 2nd century B.C. This stylized version of a kneeling man is true to its intent and not simply an unsuccessful attempt at realism. Teotihuacan Museum. (Photo Giraudon)

PRE-COLUMBIAN AMERICA

Fifteen to twenty thousand years ago, the first Asiatic colonists crossed the Bering Strait into Alaska and, following the Pacific coast, slowly made their way southward to Mexico and then Peru. The oldest stone tools found in the New World date back only 12,000 years but they already exhibit a well-developed tradition.

Striking analogies have been found between certain architectonic and decorative elements common to Asia and those used by the earliest immigrants to America. Priests of the ancient Shang dynasty in China and those of the Olmecs raised ritual mounds in the same manner and used mirrors similarly in their ceremonies. Like the Chinese, the Olmecs made animal figures, and these may also be found among the Peruvian Incas. However, since the Olmecs appeared as a definite people about 1000 B.C. and the Shang dynasty had attained dominance in China by 1523 B.C., it is therefore quite likely that the latter could have originated the customs which the first colonists carried with them.

the Olmecs

The Olmecs made their earliest American home on the tropical coast of Mexico between modern Veracruz and Tabasco. Excavations of the city of La Venta, which they built, have produced a number of very strange statues, among them a female figure whose face is divided into two juxtaposed halves, the right eye of one serving as the left eye of the other. In Mexico's National Museum, a remarkable ivory example of this theme is displayed beside a no less singular statue of a woman whose flattened head sits directly on her shoulders. Distortion like this does not imply inexperience or lack of skill, however, for the same craftsmen who produced these odd forms were also able to conquer such a rebellious and tough material as jade, as can be seen from the mask of the jaguar-god now in Boston's Peabody Museum. During the first century A.D., the Olmecs fashioned the impressive deity on the wall of the Teotihuacan Pyramid, where the mouths of the feathered serpent Quetzalcoatl alternate with the totemic image of the rain god Tlaloc. The ability to reduce these fanged jaws to a simple structure testifies to an impressive knowledge of the laws governing decorative effects, which render the plastic forms increasingly simple the farther away they are from the viewer.

The transfiguration of the human face into the ornamental emblem of Tlaloc is no less revealing. A checkerboard of cubes forms the god's formidable mouth and teeth, while the narrow forehead and cheeks, framing the tangent circles representing eyes, are treated similarly.

That the Olmecs could also produce realistic works can be seen from the bearded *Wrestler* and *Fat Child*. Both realism and abstraction were employed in the jade-encrusted wooden mask of Guerrero and, above all, the odd, clay mask of Tlatiles, whose left half sticks out its tongue and whose right half is but a barren skull.

For well over a millennium the Olmec formula was followed, and this continuity is one of the outstanding characteristics of pre-Columbian civilization. As the Olmec political system was a theocracy, the priests who derived their omnipotence from this source obviously imposed their own style on its sculpture.

the Toltecs

About 600 A.D. Teotihuacan was destroyed, either by wandering nomads or by the Toltecs, a rival tribe who had invaded the Valley of Mexico and established a capital at Tula. Their written history began in 968 when this composite community, with no culture of its own, adopted that of the defeated country. The Toltecs appeared to have accentuated the more grisly aspects of the fetishist cult. They were a caste of warriors, and the giant 15-foot statues still left in Tula show them to have been well armed. The style in this case is both dry and brutal. The single remaining facade of the Tula pyramid bears superimposed horizontal bands of wild beasts and fantastic creatures carved in bas-relief. This is essentially a graphic art, however, and far removed from the majestic sculpture of the Olmecs.

Some of the Toltecs subsequently emigrated eastward, and examples of their later style are found at Chichén-Itzá.

Giant statue of a warrior (height, 14'8''), Toltec. Basalt, 10th century A.D. This is the finest of a group of similar works found at Tula, Mexico. (Photo H. Pierre)

the Aztecs

About 1160 A.D., Tula in turn succumbed to the onslaught of the savage and warlike Chichimecs who had come down from the north. The country was subsequently chopped up into rival kingdoms of which one, the Aztec, was to impose its hegemony on Central America until the arrival of the Spanish in 1521. The Aztecs appear to have been an ethnical offshoot of the Chichimec mainstream, and they most certainly shared the Chichimec ferocity.

They worshipped the god Huitzilopochtli, who was reborn each morning thirsty for the human blood he required to defend himself against his sister the moon and his brothers the stars, night gods borne of his mother Coatlicue, the earth goddess. The Aztecs provided Huitzilopochtli amply with victims. They established their capital on an impregnable island, carefully developing its approaches, and then raided neighbouring tribes to obtain captives. For the consecration of their mighty temple in 1468, according to a reliable account, Aztec priests tore out the living hearts of 20,000 prisoners.

Yet Aztec sculpture could compete with that of the Olmecs, as can be seen from the gigantic statue of Coatlicue whose 11-ton mass was moved to the National Museum in Mexico. The dark fanatical genius of pre-Columbian art appears here in all its terrifying freedom. The earth goddess, also goddess of death, sits on two enormous griffons, her legs two twisted serpents joining to form a human face, which surmounts a carved block flanked by two appendages that serve as arms. The monster's head consists of two serpents' mouths facing one another.

This effort to inspire awe is also visible in the decoration of the alley flanking the pyramid of Tenayuca, and consisting of reptiles laid side by side. A happy opposite is the statue in Mexico's National Museum of Xochipilli, prince of flowers, also god of joy, music and dancing. Xochipilli is seated, and the stylized way of lifting his crossed legs and arms creates a very human feeling.

Aztec masks cut from such hard materials as jade and obsidian owe their fierce expressions mainly to a hideous grin.

the Zapotecs

The conquest of Central America by Huitzilopochtli's bloodthirsty worshippers met with some resistance. The Mixtecs, who lived on the western side of the mountains forming the spine of the Mexican peninsula, held out. So did the neighbouring Zapotecs, to whose brilliant imagination we owe a collection of richly decorated clay funerary urns. The seated *Scribe* of Cuilápan now in the National Museum was by the Zapotecs. Its sincerity and freedom from conventional artificiality is an obvious effort on the sculptor's part to accurately portray the sitter. Particular care was given to the face while the less personal body is treated summarily.

Masterfully decorated funerary urns may be found in private collections as well as in the Mexican National Museum. Generally, they assume the shape of a seated human being, legs crossed, surrounded by ornaments and crowned with a trophy of miscellaneous objects. Rare are the figures whose mask-like faces stand out from the background of massive forms, but they are not the least lovely, as can be seen from the urn discovered

Funerary urn showing the moon god. Zapotec. Terra-cotta, 4th to 8th century. The Zapotecs had a lively imagination for decoration, particularly that involving the human figure. National Anthropological Museum, Mexico. (Photo Giraudon)

105

at the Zapotec capital of Monte Albán, now in the National Museum. The fantastic played an important part in Zapotec art and came out mainly in their decoration of funerary urns. The urn from Teotitlán del Camino in Oaxaca has a body whose thick legs end in claws and which is surmounted by a bat's head crowned with a fluted diadem—all in all a masterpiece of imagination.

The Zapotecs could certainly be considered the most art-conscious of all the Indians. Their highly developed taste for decorative effects can perhaps best be appreciated in the geometric frieze in the priestly palace at Mitla. Here the effect is obtained by obsessively repeating a motif of sharply angled saw-toothed chevrons the length of the entire wall.

From all appearances, a distinction should be made between the arts of the Zapotecs and the Toltecs. Perhaps their high degree of civilization explains the merger between the Zapotecs and Mixtecs, which took place about 900 A.D., and the fact that the Mixtecs established their headquarters at Mitla, which had been originally built by the Zapotecs.

the Mayas

The Mayas developed a high degree of civilization on the Yucatan promontory which separates the Gulf of Campeche from the Caribbean. Though their religion also required human sacrifice, they could boast of advanced forms of ideographic writing, mathematics and astronomy. The Mayas also built step pyramids topped by temples.

Their history can conveniently be divided into two distinct periods, one running from 317 to 987 A.D. and the other from 948 to 1697. The first Mayan civilization developed in the *chiapas*, or lowlands, of present-day Guatemala, and this was also the source of the fine mask now in Mexico's National Museum.

The beautiful stele dedicated to a leader or god in Quinigua, Guatemala, was apparently erected in about 768. Almost 35 feet tall, its centre is occupied by an image of the personage in question, while the remainder is covered by a complex series of interlocking forms which nevertheless remain distinct and understandable.

Toward the end of the 6th century, the central subject began to disappear to the

nose and receding forehead, it is a physically accurate portrayal of a Mayan.

The diorite axe carved with a warrior wearing a dolphin-crested helmet, on the other hand, comes from the Veracruz region in the northern part of the Mayan Empire. The Archeological Museum in Cambridge, Mass., has a terra-cotta female head, the famous "laughing' head," which beautifully illustrates this same stylized naturalism. In short, Mayan art sought truth. The statue of a kneeling man whose head and shoulders are covered with a serape now in the Tuxtla-Gutiérrez Museum is another example of simple realism.

Vase for offerings, representing the sun god. First Mayan period, 8th to 10th century. National Anthropological Museum, Mexico. (Photo Giraudon)

benefit of the surrounding decoration and by 810 had been virtually eliminated. But that the Mayans also had a taste for naturalism can be readily seen from the *Head of a Young Man in a Plumed Headdress*, a masterpiece of Mayan classicism now owned by Mexico's Anthropological Museum. With its chiselled features, long, hooked

In extending their empire, the Mayans tended to lose the originality which set them apart from other Central American Indians. Invaded by the Toltecs during the 11th century, they regained their independence two hundred years later but seem to have lost their artistic impetus. The capital of the reconstituted empire, when excavated, yielded nothing more than shoddy undecorated buildings. When the Conquistadors finally landed, they encountered only the Aztec civilization, which they soon devastated.

Vase in the form of a human head. Mochican. Painted terracotta, about 500 B.C. The first immigrants to Peru modelled vases with human faces of great strength and scant details. (Photo Giraudon)

PERU

The Pacific coast of South America and what is now Peru were first peopled around 11,000 B.C. by immigrants who had slowly filtered down from Central America and Mexico. They were hunters, food gatherers and makers of primitive pottery, a few remains of which have been unearthed. Not until about 2500 B.C. did they succeed in domesticating such local animals as the llama and the alpaca. Since they found the land inhospitable, they scattered into independent colonies between steep mountains and forbidding deserts; and this isolation accounts for their separate evolution.

the Chavins

In the 9th century B.C., a tribe called the Chavins occupied the northern plateaus, and constructed a temple at Chavin de Huantar with huge blocks of stone. This temple housed their "great idol," a white granite monolith over fifteen feet high whose surface is carved in relief with interlocking curves—from all appearances, it is a representation of a human being with jaguar teeth. Carved on the lintel of the temple gate is a relief of birds with outstretched wings, clearly discernible despite an almost geometric stylization.

The Chavins' formal approach to sculpture continued over the next five hundred years. Their favourite subjects were jaguars and condors. All the reliefs were executed by carving out the background. That the Chavins also made sculpture in the round can be seen from the few isolated heads that have been found. The fact that their necks were fitted with pegs shows that they were meant to be attached to separate bodies.

About 500 B.C. the Chavins gave way to the Mochicas, and a mighty civilization developed later in this area.

the Mochicas

The Mochicas built towering pyramids topped by temples dedicated to the sun and moon. Large sculpture was unknown to them, but they engaged in the minor arts, especially ceramics, with consummate skill. Many portrait urns of acute realism and incomparable breadth of style have come down to us. Equally talented as goldsmiths, the Mochicas sculpted a beautiful puma of gold whose belly forms a bag. Its entire body is decorated with raised geometric representations of a double-headed serpent.

the Incas

The Chimus continued the Mochican civilization, decorating the walls of their temples with alternating ornamental figures, stylized animals and, above all, birds. About 600 A.D. the Chimus fell before the invasion of a people who came from the south. These people had their main temple at Tiahuanaco, at an altitude of 12,645 feet, in the present area of western Bolivia, and are regarded as precursors of the Incas.

Under their leader Pachacutec, the Incas finally unified the Andean region into a single dominion toward the middle of the 15th century. An able diplomat as well as a conqueror, Pachacutec established a South American empire similar in scope to Alexander's. The Incas' artistic talents flourished mainly in architecture and the minor arts, particularly ceramics. They did, however, carve small objects from hard stone, such as alpacas with depressions in their backs to receive offerings. From all the evidence, monumental sculpture was unknown to the Incas, whose civilization foundered under the Spanish invasion of the early 16th century.

OCEANIA

The Pacific contains thousands of islands and atolls, the largest of which—except for the continent of Australia—are New Guinea and New Zealand. The former is the centre of the Melanesian culture, while the latter lies far to the south. These islands received their population from the west, probably China, and the process appears to have taken many centuries. Bone and chipped stone tools and implements dating back to the seventh millennium B.C. have been found in New Guinea, but the more distant islands seem not to have been populated until the first few millennia before Christ. Evidently the last wave of immigrants to this vast territory sailed in from Asia via the Philippines, the Moluccas and Celebes. These peoples intermingled, and some of them attained a high degree of civilization, as their art shows.

Melanesian art was magical in intent. Representations of the human figure were supposed to provide the dead with a repository for their *mana*, spirits who governed after-life and could be either benevolent or evil. Conse-

quently, it became necessary to propitiate *mana* with appropriate gifts and according to a carefully planned ritual. Also worshipped were innumerable tribal deities, or *atua*, and a whole roster of household gods, the *oromatua*. To these the Melanesians and Polynesians dedicated fetishes and masks, in which animal and distorted human forms probably had some religious significance.

Oceanic artists chose to misrepresent nature. Invariably they distorted the human face, the eyes being slanted, the nose hooked into a beak or stretched to trunk-like proportions, the mouth made frighteningly hideous with wild boar tusks. Caricature was not the aim of such monstrosities; they all had a mystical or magical meaning. Viewing such works, many of which are superbly executed, it would appear that the greater the travesty of nature, the greater the protective power. Imagination was a law unto itself in this field.

Oceanic art may be conveniently divided into three major areas: Polynesia, Melanesia (the largest and most varied) and Micronesia (which includes the Caroline and Mariana islands). In the latter, true sculpture did not exist, art being characterized by an extreme simplicity in which the human head became an egg-shaped mass.

New Guinea and the New Hebrides ranked as the two major centres of Oceanic art. Stone was sometimes employed, but more often the roots of giant ferns. In addition to totem masks, carving was applied mainly to the prows of canoes, ceremonial pillars, the ridgepoles of huts and the reliefs inside each village's "house of spirits," which was reserved exclusively for magical incantations. Often fantastic interpretations of the human head mingle with interlocking motifs of incredible intricacy and considerable beauty.

Polynesia, which covers the Marquesas, Tuamotu and Hawaii, also extends as far south as Easter Island. In the British Museum there is a fine Hawaiian statue of a temple guardian whose mask-like features are tortured into an expression of fantastic ferocity.

The famed colossal heads of Easter Island, crudely carved from volcanic stone, apparently marked the site of a religious centre, as they, too, represented ancestral spirits. These great statues were sculpted by the most primitive means, as metals were unknown in Oceania before the advent of the Europeans.

Ancestral mask, New Guinea. Painted wood. The Asiatic immigrants to the Pacific Islands made startling masks which completely transformed facial features. (Photo A. Held)

111

Human mask, West Africa. Wood. Naturalistic portraits are rare in African art. Most sculpture tends toward stylized symbols. (Photo A. Held)

Human head, Ifé culture, Central Africa. Terra-cotta. Traditions lasted for centuries in Africa, making art works hard to date precisely. (Photo A. Held)

AFRICA

Few man-made objects produced prior to the 16th century have come down to us from Africa, where the climate plays havoc with such perishable materials as wood. Nevertheless, what has been recovered sheds considerable light on the aesthetics of native black societies.

African artisans worked to order, practising a craft which they had learned from a recognized master. African art is not the expression of individual talent, for sculptors referred only to a repertory of forms which had been previously established and approved by the local cult.

They were not even permitted the choice of which wood to use, but had to employ that chosen by the priests, since the figure to be carved, as well as the tree from which it came, participated in the vital force emanating from the tribe's titular deity.

African sculptors did not attempt individualized portraits of their sitters. If they wished to portray a certain illustrious leader, they did so by accentuating some personal and distinguishing characteristic. The sculptor's essential aim was to capture the vital inherited essence that gave his subject life. However, it was not the statue itself which possessed this magic virtue; the statue could only receive it from a medicine man, or *nyanga*, invested with the divine spirit. Consequently, a worn-out or damaged mask could be discarded without inconvenience. It could be easily replaced by another, which a religious ceremony would endow with the same magical properties.

This explains the uniform similarity of these works. The mask itself is but a symbol expressing an idea. Nevertheless, African sculptors loved their craft and took keen satisfaction in decorating not only masks and statues but even the tools and implements they were asked to produce—for example, the pestle whose handle was carved by a Baluba sculptor into the shape of a young woman's head (Rietberg Museum, Zurich).

African sculpture flourished in two major regions, the Bambara Sudan and the Baoulé Benin, with centres at Esie, Ife and Nok. The first is noted for its decorative imagination, as shown in its stylized long-horn antelopes; the second for its realism, best illustrated by a beautiful 16th century ivory female mask now in the British Museum. Stone was seldom used in Africa, but fine bronzes were cast. Forged iron proved very effective.

The whole concept of composition remained foreign to African sculptors. On the bronze door in the Abidjan Museum, Ivory Coast, the components of its commemorative decoration are all arranged on the same vertical plane. Only after the arrival of the Europeans did African sculptors produce the marvellous plates showing the chief *Oba* accompanied by two vassals, now in the British Museum.

from the middle ages to the renaissance | 4

After the break-up of the Roman Empire upon the death of Theodosius the Great in 395 A.D., only the eastern or Byzantine part managed to keep any semblance of imperial power, and Rome itself foundered under repeated attacks from invading barbarians. In the midst of Europe's dark and confused anarchy, only the Church stood fast as a bulwark of unity and culture, and at the end of the 8th century, Charlemagne reestablished the western imperial tradition in creating a civilization which leaned heavily on it.

Two basic trends began to appear: a return to natural forms, and more emphasis on the human figure so dear to the Graeco-Roman tradition. There was also a drift toward realism, from the earliest primitive Romanesque sculpture to the refined masterpieces of high Gothic.

From the Carolingian Renaissance to the humanistic Renaissance of 16th century Italy, God was all-important—both the ultra-powerful Jehovah of the Last Judgement, as depicted by Romanesque sculptors, and the compassionate deity of the Gothic masters. It was to honour God and show Him to the people that the great medieval cathedrals, the "sermons in stone," were built. "Stone was the material of the high Middle Ages, even when camouflaged in polychrome, and constituted the framework as well as the building's decoration." (H. Focillon)

The Handsome God. Stone, about 1230. Pier of the main door, Amiens Cathedral. Its noble drapery and majestic pose are outstanding. (Photo A. Allemand)

BYZANTIUM

In the course of the 4th century, the Roman Empire gradually disintegrated. In 323 Constantine the Great (274–337) chose the colony of Byzantium for his future capital of Constantinople, and when, in 476, the imperial regalia moved there, it marked the eclipse of the Western Empire by the Eastern.

Oriental leanings which had prevailed in Rome for many centuries became further entrenched by the move to the new capital and by ever more contacts with the people of the Middle East. In sculpture the realistic, three-dimensional treatment of volume lost out to an abstract decorative art in which themes were developed on a single flat plane.

Major sculpture woefully declined from the 4th to the 6th century, the only significant examples being the sarcophagi found at Arles in southern France, and in Spain, Rome and Asia Minor. Realistic themes, too, felt the impact of the East, the beardless Christ of the Hellenistic tradition being replaced by luxuriantly bearded Syrian versions. Little by little, purely decorative scrolls and ornamental tracery virtually wiped out any pictorial representation, and this movement continued until the reign of Justinian.

Reminders of the ancient world's naturalist tradition still appeared in the minor arts, though even here the themes had been transposed and adapted to the new religion.

Capital from the church of San Vitale, Ravenna. 6th century. Abstract patterns predominate in spite of the rampant animal figures at the top. (Photo Scala)

Christ crowning Romanus and Eudoxius. Ivory, 10th century. The borrowings from the goldsmith's art are obvious. Medal Collection, Bibliothèque Nationale, Paris. (Photo Ségalat)

In 726, Emperor Leo III the Isaurian published an edict against images, setting off the iconoclast controversy which was to spark untold riots and a sacrilegious destruction, and which was not really to come to an end until the 9th century with the advent of the Macedonian dynasty.

By this time, two conflicting schools could be seen in Byzantine sculpture: the imperial art which hewed to the tradition of ancient Rome, and a monastic art catering to the purely Byzantine taste for austere abstraction. Nevertheless, the iconoclastic schism definitively established the victory of colour over form, so that sculpture had to seek refuge among the minor arts. Thus, thanks to the Crusades, Byzantine themes and decorative language influenced the West for many years and ended only with the fall of Byzantium to the Ottoman Turks in 1453.

INFLUENCE OF THE BARBARIANS

From the 2nd century A.D. onward, hordes of barbarians, attracted by Italy's wealth, invaded southern Europe. In independent tribes and groups, they swarmed over the whole continent: Alemans, Burgundians and Franks in Gaul; the Vandals in Spain; first the Visigoths (who occupied Rome in 410), then the Ostrogoths and finally the Lombards in Italy.

Living an essentially nomadic existence and thus concentrating on the minor arts, the barbarians possessed age-old links with Mesopotamian civilization. These gave them a profound taste for abstract curvilinear stylization and interlocking forms.

In Italy, the barbarians' abstract decorative sculpture merged into and even accelerated the natural development of Byzantine art.

Figurative elements in their work consisted mainly of fantastic stylized animals like dragons and chimeras. Portrayals of the human figure, though copied from Roman originals, were schematically carved, mainly in low relief and only occasionally in the round.

Prow of a ship. Wood, 9th century. Its decoration tends toward complete abstraction. Antiquities Museum, University of Oslo.

INFLUENCE OF ISLAM

The Arab conquest of the Mediterranean basin began shortly after Mohammed's death in 632 and was only stopped in France by Charles Martel's unexpected victory at Poitiers in 732. In Spain, however, the struggle against Arab occupation continued until 1492.

Art in the newly conquered territories was strongly influenced by Byzantium and Sassanid Persia. Furthermore, Moslem religious doctrines accentuated the long-standing Semitic prejudice against representing the human figure. Realistic sculpture cropped up here and there, but found small favour because of the Middle East's inherent fondness for abstraction. Sculpture on the whole was relegated to the minor arts, where much fine work was done in ceramics, ivory, wood, and metals. Real or imaginary beasts carved on brass censers and ewers reflect the persistence of ancient Persian traditions.

Decorative sculpture as an integral part of architecture, on the other hand, flourished. Interlocking designs and ornamental scrolls similar to those of the Byzantine and barbarian canon reappear, and a new and meaningful decorative motif is added— the Arabs' beautiful cursive script.

Ivory casket. Spanish, 10th century. The line of Kufic script around the bottom of the cover typifies contemporary Islamic influence. Louvre, Paris. (Photo Boudot-Lamotte)

119

BEGINNINGS OF ROMANESQUE SCULPTURE

Charlemagne (768–814) established a vast empire which far outstripped the territory actually held by the Franks, and his defence of the papacy against the Lombards earned him the honour of being crowned emperor in Rome on Christmas Day, 800 A.D. His reign saw the birth of a real European civilization, which aimed at renewing its ties with the past in every cultural form.

Monumental sculpture hardly existed in the Carolingian era, since the period's basic architectural decoration consisted of Byzantine-inspired mosaics or mural paintings. Sculpture in ivory or metals, on the other hand, won high popularity and these so-called minor arts enjoyed a true renaissance in sculpture and carving in the round.

As early as the 10th century, several factors contributed to the birth and dissemination of true Romanesque art. They included the growth and increasing power of the great monastic orders, who spread the same culture throughout Europe; pilgrimages to Jerusalem, Rome and Santiago de Compostela; the conquest of England

and Sicily by the Normans, who superimposed western European traditions onto existing native arts; the Great Schism of 1050 between the Catholic and Orthodox churches, marking the ultimate split of the two civilizations founded by Rome; and finally, at the end of the 11th century, the Crusades.

Eleventh century monumental sculpture in stone was strongly affected by the minor arts, drawing its main inspiration from relief techniques employed in metalwork, ivory carving and painting. A wealth of decorative elements harmoniously combined animal and vegetable themes with purely geometric motifs. Sculpture was freely adapted and bent to fit essentially religious architectural frames without the slightest concern for the realism of volumes or lines. However, this form of decoration was applied to only a few vital parts of these buildings: pediments, lintels and column capitals.

Statue-reliquary of Saint Foy. Wood covered with gold leaf, inset with gems and cameos, late 9th century. From the treasury of the church of Sainte-Foy-de-Conques, Aveyron department. The statue's pose is rigorously frontal and many of its components were later additions. (Photo Giraudon)

Angel. Marble bas-relief, late 11th century, from the choir screen of Saint Sernin cathedral in Toulouse. The figure is brought out by means of shallow undercutting. Its curly hair and toga-like garment are Gallo-Roman in inspiration, though its composition reflects contemporary metalwork. (Photo J. P. Vieil)

ROMANESQUE FRANCE

Romanesque-style sculpture reached its apogee in the 12th century when the establishment of strong centralized monarchies and a period of relative peace encouraged the development of local workshops and schools. The finest examples of Romanesque sculpture were produced in France, where several distinct schools developed.

Languedoc

In this region the main centre of Romanesque art was Toulouse, where Pope Urban II consecrated the altar in the choir of Saint Sernin in 1096. Only four years later, work began on the magnificent abbey of Saint-Pierre de Moissac. Sculptural talent flowered in this region during the first half of the 12th century, producing a plethora of masterpieces at Carennac, Cahors, Beaulieu, Souillac

The Prophet Isaiah. Stone, about 1130–1140, from the portal of the church in Souillac, Lot department. This elongated figure with its flowing hair and beard is typical of Romanesque sculpture in southwestern France. (Photo Boudot-Lamotte)

and elsewhere. Figures (saints, prophets and other Old Testament characters) are invariably elongated no matter what the pose. Flowing hair and beards fall into long tresses.

The Last Judgement. Stone, about 1130–1140. West pediment of Saint Lazarus cathedral in Autun. The lintel bears the artist's signature: *Gislebertus hoc fecit.* (Photo Verroust)

Burgundy

The most productive sites in this area were at Saint Lazarus in Autun and the Church of La Madeleine in Vézelay, where a series of superb story-telling capitals and vast sculptured pediments were executed between 1120 and 1140. Clothing, moulded almost skin-tight to the body in fine pleats and folds, appears wind-swept. Again the general lines are exaggeratedly elongated, the poses excessively twisted, to give the whole a feeling of life and movement.

Auvergne

Auvergne was one of the first French provinces to rediscover the technique of carving in the round—probably because, being far from major highways, it clung to Gallo-Roman principles. Though the style is frequently squat and heavy, everyday scenes are realistically portrayed, with capital carvings often highlighted by paintings. Reliquary statues, many of them of the Virgin and inspired by the magnificent *Saint Foy* of Conques, multiplied during the 12th century.

north of the Loire

Little or no Romanesque sculpture appeared north of the Loire River, for the Gothic influence made its first entry at Saint-Denis as early as 1140. In Normandy, on the other hand, where Romanesque architecture reached a peak about this time, decorative elements remained basically geometric.

Poitou

In western France, in Poitou, it was only natural that Islamic influence held strong, because of continuous contact with Spain. Here sculpture appeared later than in Languedoc or Burgundy, and the vast pediments were ignored in favour of arches and capitals.

The Massacre of the Innocents. Mid-12th century. Coving of the western portal of Sainte Marie-des-Dames cathedral in Saintes, France. Lack of pediments led sculptors to carve the covings. (Photo Verroust)

Provence

The Provençal school of sculpture also started late, about 1140, and lingered into the early years of the 13th century. Deeply inspired by the many fragments of antique sculpture found locally, it is in many ways comparable to contemporary works in northern Italy. This may be clearly seen at Saint-Gilles-du-Gard (1178–1180) and at Saint-Trophime in Arles (1190–1200).

ROMANESQUE SPAIN

Romanesque art also gained a foothold in Catalonia and the kingdoms of northwestern Spain during the 11th century. Here local rulers appealed to the monks for help in their endless wars against the Moors, and Santiago de Compostela, the pilgrims' goal, became one of Christendom's most important shrines.

In spite of some quite original local traits, the influence of French Romanesque sculpture, particularly of the Languedoc school, can be clearly recognized at Santiago and Leon. Two masterpieces of Spanish Romanesque sculpture are the goldsmiths' portal at Santiago de Compostela and the door of the south transept in Leon Cathedral. Also worth noting is the deep imprint of Arabic art, whose elements decorate much chased silver and goldwork. Undoubtedly the most famous of these is the *Arca Santa* presented to Oviedo Cathedral by Alfonso VI in 1075. Mozarab craftsmen also left their stamp on southern French sculpture—testimony to cultural exchanges between France and Spain.

Capital at San Pedro, Roda, Catalonia. Stone, 11th century. Still elementary, the decoration includes geometrical and floral elements typical of Romanesque art. (Photo Mas)

ROMANESQUE ITALY

The techniques of Romanesque architecture were readily adopted in Italy.

Lombardy

Wiligelmo, who worked in Lombardy during the first half of the 12th century, was largely responsible for renewed local interest in this art. Until then, deeply imbued by the strictures of Byzantine art and the barbarian art of the Lombards, Italian sculptors had neglected the human figure to concentrate almost exclusively on linear decoration or stylized animals. An inscription on the facade of Modena's cathedral reveals that as early as 1099 Wiligelmo had executed a series of bas-reliefs set into its walls. Their exquisite lines, sobriety of representation and sense of plastic values unmistakeably show his penchant for the antique. Wiligelmo cast a long shadow in northern and central Italy and his works may also be found in the cathedrals of Nonantola, Cremona and Verona.

Benedetto Antelami dominated the second half of the 12th century. Born in Genoa about 1150, he worked mainly in Parma, where in 1178 he executed a masterful *Deposition* for the city's cathedral. A hint of the Byzantine may be seen in the hieratic poses of the figures standing out

The Creation of Adam and Eve, by Wiligelmo. Bas-relief, early 12th century. Modena Cathedral. Wiligelmo treated traditional subjects firmly and realistically. (Photo Scala)

from a background of abstract arabesques, as well as in the composition's rigid symmetry. Yet the rendering of the volumes gives this work a monumental quality, while anecdotal and realistic details breathe life into it. Antelami also worked on three porches of the Parma baptistery where construction began in 1196. Here his muse changed and he showed a style far more flexible and free than in his *Deposition*.

Antelami's influence was great and can be seen in the calendar of the months at Ferrara's cathedral as well as in the prophets of the church at Fidenza. This influence, or at least the spirit which infused the works of Antelami, also manifests itself in contemporary Venetian works

Tuscany

Tuscan sculptors gleaned much from the Lombard school, but without losing their originality; and in the latter half of the 12th century Bonanno introduced bronze techniques inspired by German works. As Bonanno's entire Pisan output has disappeared, we have only his fabulous bronze doors, done in 1186 for the cathedral of Monreale in Sicily, to show his happy blend—both in design and execution—of antique and Byzantine traditions.

Deposition from the Cross, by Benedetto Antelami, 1178. Parma Cathedral. The rigorously geometrical composition of this bas-relief is accentuated by the hieratic poses of its figures. (Photo Scala)

ROMANESQUE ART
IN THE GERMANIC COUNTRIES

On the other side of the Rhine, the Ottonian dynasty put an end to the troubles which followed the demise of the Carolingian Empire. Otto I (912–973) restored imperial dignity and encouraged the classically inspired culture.

Germanic civilization flourished as a result, and it was this artistic renaissance, with sculpture in the lead, which produced the burnished gold altar ornaments which Henry II donated to the Basle cathedral in 1020, a great work, simple in composition yet refined in execution.

The antique influence shows itself again in bronzes cast

Altar decoration from Basle Cathedral. Gold, between 1014 and 1022. A gift of Emperor Henry II, it is now in the Cluny Museum, Paris. (Normandy Photo)

at Hildesheim under the auspices of Bishop Bernward. Indeed, the Christ Column of Hildesheim is an obvious transposition of Trajan's famed column in Rome.

Although magnificent examples of Romanesque architecture abound in the German-speaking nations, the same cannot be said, unfortunately, of sculpture in stone. Such sculpture remained relatively unpopular as a form of expression, even for decoration.

FLEMISH ROMANESQUE

Flemish sculpture also found glorious fulfillment in the art of working metals. Coppersmiths had shops in several towns along the valleys of the Scheldt and the Meuse.

Between 1111 and 1118, the master artisan Rénier de Huy executed the celebrated bronze baptismal fonts of the church of Saint Bartholomew in Liège. Godefroid, another Huy artisan, became equally celebrated for metalwork, his fame spreading as far afield as France, Britain and the Germanic countries. Toward the end of the 12th century, the Meuse school of sculpture produced Nicholas de Verdun, the most celebrated of whose metal and enamel altarpieces are now displayed at Klosterneubourg near Vienna, Austria. His advanced style could almost be considered Gothic.

Metalwork obviously had a tremendous influence on Flemish stone sculpture, yet the artistic trends coming north from Burgundy, Languedoc and even Byzantium were also felt, as can be seen from the 12th century *Dom Rupert Virgin* now in Liège.

The Baptism of Christ, by Renier de Huy. Cast copper, about 1107–1118. Detail from the baptismal fonts in Saint Bartholomew, Liège. (Photo J. P. Vieil)

12th AND 13th CENTURIES IN FRANCE

Around the middle of the 12th century there appeared at Saint-Denis, near Paris, a new architectural style based on vaults built over crossed ogives. It was called Gothic or ogival.

As this style developed, sculpture gradually lost its purely decorative role and was increasingly subjected to a rigid architectural frame. Even the iconography itself changed, so that the Romanesque standard repertory of monsters and stylized leaves

---

The Labours of the Months. Stone, about 1200–1215. Western portal of Senlis Cathedral. Though the artist's technique is still clumsy, his sense of observation is exceptionally keen. (Photo S. Vaucher)

disappeared in favour of a more realistic treatment of nature. In addition, sculpture was almost wholly relegated to the outside of churches. The placing of subjects gained in importance and followed a system of strict rules and customs. Christ had the primary place on the central pier, flanked by Apostles on both jambs of the portals, while the Last Judgement occupied the pediment above.

One of the lateral doors was always reserved for the Virgin holding the Child in her arms and the prophets who had forecast the Messiah's coming, as well as characters who had figured in scenes preceding the Saviour's birth. The portal of the other tran-

sept was usually dedicated to the patron saint of the church or locality. Outer walls between the portals pictured charming scenes of day-to-day life, those in calendars showing the labours of the months. During the 13th century the main pediment was frequently allocated to the Virgin.

Symbolism taught the faithful vital meanings and values of the holy texts. Certain famous figures are always represented in the same fashion. For instance, a partly bald Saint Peter, with a short curly beard, inevitably toys with keys. Furthermore, by a subtle system of parallels, Old Testament figures evoke those in the New: Melchizedek offering bread to Abraham suggests Jesus giving communion to the Apostles.

The meanings of these sculptures had to be accessible to all, and this, combined with their accomplished techniques and profound faith, enabled Gothic sculptors to attain the highest summits of artistic expression.

The Gilded Virgin. Stone, about 1270. Main portal of Amiens Cathedral. This broadly carved statue is notable mainly for its fine pose and gently tempered realism. (Photo Giraudon)

the royal portals

The typical Gothic portal with its three doors, pediments and columnar statues on the jambs first appeared in Saint-Denis. In 1145, upon completion of the work there commissioned by Abbot Suger, the same sculptors moved to Chartres, where they executed the royal portal of that city's cathedral. There, the right hand pediment is devoted to the Nativity, the left to the Ascension and the centre to the Last Judgement. Column statues represent Old Testament patriarchs and prophets. The style of these rather resembles contemporary Romanesque works in Languedoc and Burgundy, with excessive elongation, chiselled drapery treatment and stiffness of pose; but naturalism softens the facial expressions and gives each statue an individual personality.

The royal portals of Chartres and Saint-Denis had many imitators elsewhere in France: at Etampes, Le Mans, Paris and Saint-Loup-de-Naud.

The Queen of Sheba. Stone, late 12th century. Column statue from Notre Dame in Corbeil. In spite of its elongation, the treatment of the face and drapery shows an obvious attempt at realism. (Photo Giraudon)

the great cathedrals

The period between 1190 and the end of the 13th century saw construction of the greatest French cathedrals.

At **Chartres,** the strict iconographic programme laid out originally continued throughout the 13th century, although a more flexible and freely expressed style evolved. The north and south facades were worked on alternately between 1200 and 1260. The north portal deals with the Virgin and the Old Testament, the south portal being devoted to the Last Judgement and the New Testament. On the south transept (Portal of the Martyrs), Saint Theodore appears as a typical knight of Saint Louis' time. His noble expression, the accurate treatment of his clothing, and the way the statue stands out from the column— all show the progress achieved in the hundred years since the first columnar statues of Saint-Denis.

Saint Theodore. Stone, about 1240. Portal of the Martyrs, Chartres Cathedral. The proportions of this figure and its broadly carved drapery testify to the skill and artistry of Chartres' sculptors. (Photo Boudot-Lamotte)

The Angel of Saint Nicaise. Stone, late 12th century. Facade of Reims Cathedral. It is typical of the works produced by the cathedral's most original school of sculptors. (Photo Boudot-Lamotte)

Notre Dame de Paris possesses a north transept (1250) with a serenity and grandeur equal to that of Chartres. The Virgin with Child on the pier distributes her weight slightly more on one leg, and the rich, heavy folds of the enveloping drapery give the whole a remarkably refined elegance. Comparable purity and beauty can be found only in the statues of Christ teaching, of which the finest example is the *Beau Dieu* of Amiens (1225).

Amiens Cathedral has a facade, completed in a short time (1225–1236), showing perfect homogeneity of design and execution, in accordance with an ideal iconographic pattern.

Reims. An original proposal for the facade at Reims was conceived in 1210–1215, but these projects came to naught, and work continued through the 13th century. This was perhaps the culmination of Gothic sculpture, with carving no longer limited to portals but spreading over the entire facade. Various scenes from the Virgin's life, executed in different styles by several schools of sculptors, were imitated all across Europe. Reims was the very last of the magnificent Gothic cathedrals, and later monuments such as Bourges and Strasbourg modestly took their cue from their great predecessors.

Tomb of Louis de France, son of Saint Louis (Louis IX). About 1260. Now in Saint-Denis basilica but originally at Royaumont abbey. (Photo Ségelat)

funerary sculpture

Religious sculpture was far and away the most important form; its themes were frequently repeated in the minor arts of gold and ivory. Next in popularity came funerary sculpture. Sarcophagi bearing recumbent figures reposed in gloomy splendour in niches or in isolated parts of cathedrals. Some were in bronze, as can be seen from the tombs of Evrard de Fouilloy (d. 1222) in the Louvre and Geoffroy d'Eu (d. 1236) in Amiens Cathedral. In 1263, Saint Louis decided to move the remains of former French kings to Saint-Denis, and for this purpose he commissioned 16 horizontal figures to honour the Carolingian and Merovingian dynasties as well as the early Capetians.

The Margrave Uta. Stone, late 13th century. Naumburg Cathedral. One of a group of lay figures whose presence in a cathedral was exceptional at that time. (Photo Boudot-Lamotte)

The Synagogue. Red granite, about 1230. From Strasbourg Cathedral and clearly inspired by works on the north portal of Chartres, it is now in the Musée de l'Oeuvre, Strasbourg.

13th CENTURY GERMANY

Master sculptors of foreign origin first appeared in Germany around the start of the 13th century. Their use of stone caused a fantastic development in this medium at a time when traditional work in bronze continued.

Bamberg. The stone relief choir screen in the Bamberg cathedral, executed about 1230, shows no foreign influence. Set in pairs, figures are well separated from their background and the material is treated with tremendous expression and energy. The rather aggressive character of these works is softened by the purely decorative treatment of drapery. Contrasting with this entirely original work is that of a master, undoubtedly trained at Reims, who subsequently went to Bamberg. The moving yet sober style of the *Visitation* he executed for the cathedral bears the stamp of Reims.

Another series of sculptures in the Bamberg cathedral reveals the presence of a truly unique artist. Inside the building, statues of its twelve founders—eight men and four women—grace the choir area. Probably executed between 1250 and 1260, these works have absolutely no architectural function. Although they are retrospective portraits, their individuality and realism do not exclude a certain majesty.

Strasbourg. While Bamberg's second group of sculptors turned to Reims for their inspiration, Strasbourg's early carvers borrowed from Chartres—introducing in the process a new partnership of strength and elegance. Beautiful examples in this cathedral are the masterful carvings of the *Church* and the *Synagogue*. Later Strasbourg sculptors (1280–1290) worked on the western facade in a far livelier style. Drapery folds are deeper, stances of the figures more exaggerated and their faces are rapt and intense. The famous group of the *Wise and Foolish Virgins* typify a tendency toward expressionism which was to become increasingly apparent in German art of the 14th and 15th centuries.

The tradition of bronze sculpture at **Hildesheim** continued throughout the 13th century, producing such exquisite examples as the baptismal fonts cast for the cathedral about 1230.

13th CENTURY SPAIN

Like its Romanesque sculpture, Spain's Gothic sculpture originated at Santiago de Compostela; it did so in 1183 when Master Mathieu added the Porch of Glory to the Romanesque basilica. Only the central pediment is carved, showing Christ the Judge surrounded by the symbols of the evangelists, while, in the splays, column statues represent prophets and apostles. The portals of both the Avila cathedral and the Camara Santa in Oviedo drew their inspiration from the Porch of Glory.

For the Spanish, the 13th century was a period of dazzling brilliance. Their 1212 victory over the Arabs at Las Navas de Tolosa ushered in the merger of the kingdoms of Leon and Castile in 1230. The era's two great products were the cathedrals of Burgos and Leon.

The White Virgin. Stone, 13th century. Facade of Leon Cathedral. The squat appearance and accentuated realism are typically Spanish. (Photo J. Roubier)

Burgos. Bishop Maurice laid the cornerstone of Burgos cathedral in 1221 but not until 1240 did Master Henri, a mason of the French school of Champagne, take over. The door of the Apostles on the north transept, whose pediment shows the Last Judgement, closely resembles the style of the north portal of Reims except that the treatment is more massive; the same could be said of its southern counterpart, the "Sarmental" door.

Burgos' influence, uniquely regional, is seen in the little cathedral of El Burgo de Osma and at Leon. Indeed, for the portals of the transepts at Leon, Master Henri simply duplicated those that he had done at Burgos. The portals on the western facade, on the other hand, are pale imitations of Chartres and other cathedrals of northern and central France (Reims, Amiens, Bourges) without, unfortunately, achieving similar grandeur. On the left-hand pier, the *White Virgin* statue recalls the *Gilded Virgin* of Amiens.

A Prophet. Stone, late 12th century. From the Porch of Glory, Santiago de Compostela. The influence of sculptors from Burgundy and Aquitaine is obvious. (Photo Ségalat)

13th CENTURY ITALY

In the 13th century, Italian art, and particularly sculpture, remained aloof from Gothicism, with a return to the antique which heralded the magnificent Renaissance of the Quattrocento (15th century).

Nicolas Pisano, (c. 1220–1287). The sculptural works of Nicolas Pisano of Tuscany clearly reflect this independence. His Pisan products were obviously inspired by classical examples, the baptistery pulpit being decorated with bas-reliefs separated by small columns topped with Corinthian capitals, while the font is supported by caryatids. In his bas-reliefs of the *Nativity*, the Virgin's reclining pose, costume and drapery are all taken from ancient statues of Roman matrons.

Giovanni Pisano (1250–1314). Son of Nicolas Pisano, this sculptor used even more antique motifs in the magnificent pulpits he executed for San

The Adoration of the Magi, by Nicolas Pisano. Marble, about 1260. Detail from the pulpit of the baptistery, Pisa. This work is clearly inspired by classical sculpture. (Photo Scala)

Andrea de Pistoia (1299–1301) and Pisa's cathedral (1302–1310). At the same time, however, he added a new dramatic flair and a realism and movement lacking in his father's work.

Arnolfo di Cambio (c. 1240–1302). The same vigour, intensity of expression and the same predilection for sharply defined volumes enlivened the art of Arnolfo di Cambio, a pupil of Nicolas Pisano who was both architect and sculptor. He worked for Charles of Anjou for a time in Rome and then continued his career in Siena, Perugia and Bologna. Commissions for fountains, tombs and ciboria enabled him to exercise his talents as both sculptor and architect simultaneously. The geometrical rigidity of both the frame and volume of his compositions sometimes results in considerable aridity, mainly in the way the folds in his draperies regularly break into a V-shape.

By harking back to the ancient tradition, Nicolas and Giovanni Pisano, as well as Arnolfo di Cambio, opened the way to a new conception of sculpture which combined intensity of expression with a human scale.

Kneeling figure, by Arnolfo di Cambio. About 1278. Detail from a fountain in Perugia. (Photo Scala)

14th CENTURY FRANCE

The serious financial crisis which began in France after Saint Louis' death in 1270, and which worsened after Philip the Good's succession in 1285, led to a temporary halt in cathedral building, so that sculpture thus lost its monumental purpose. Recurring wars and the schism which led to the papal exile in Avignon did, however, induce artists to travel more, and this created a pan-European international style.

The religious idealism of the 13th century gave way to a new spiritual trend reflected by an ambivalent attitude toward death as well as a sentimental, mystical devotion to the Virgin and a host of patron saints. Hence three types of sculpture grew popular: statues of the Virgin and Child, statues of the saints, and funerary monuments.

During the 14th century, the king of France and his vassals, the great feudal lords, frequently imported artists from Flanders. Count-

Virgin and Child, known as the Jeanne d'Evreux Virgin. Vermeil, 14th century. Louvre, Paris. (Photo Giraudon)

ess Mahaut of Artois, for instance, called in Jean Pepin de Huy; and the great patron Charles V employed two of the foremost contemporary sculptors: André Beauneveu de Valenciennes and Jean de Liège. The latter executed several notable tombs and had a hand in decorating the Louvre's spiral staircase with statues.

In 1364, Charles V commissioned André Beauneveu (born c. 1330) to carve his tomb as well as one for his wife, his father, John the Good, and grandfather, Philippe de Valois. After a spell with the Count of Flanders, Beauneveu went to work for the king's brother, the Duke de Berry, starting in 1386 and collaborating with other Flemish artists like Jean de Huy to produce statues and illuminations. The miniatures Beauneveu painted for the Duke de Berry's psalter rank among the art masterpieces of all ages.

Among the most celebrated works of sculpture executed during Charles V's reign is the *Great Pillar* in Amiens Cathedral which Cardinal Lagrange had embellished with statues of the king, his heir, the dauphin, and his councilor, Bureau de la Rivière.

Bureau de la Rivière. Stone, 14th Century. Amiens Cathedral. The flexible drapery and treatment of the face exemplify the discreet realism typical of the 14th century. (Photo J. Vieil)

14th CENTURY BURGUNDY AND FLANDERS

After the death of Charles V in 1380, artists tended to forsake the court of his mad successor, Charles VI, and to seek work with the latter's luxury-loving uncles, the dukes of Berry, Burgundy and Orleans.

The Well of Moses, by Claus Sluter. About 1400–1406. From the former Charterhouse of Champmol, Dijon. (Photo Verroust)

Art flourished in Burgundy during the 14th century. The fact that the dukes of Burgundy had managed to assemble a vast jigsaw of holdings (including Artois, Hainaut and Flanders) through marriage or inheritance meant that Flemish artists could work in Dijon under the patronage of the same lord. In addition, the diplomatic talent of four successive dukes spared Burgundy from the horrors of war for many years.

When Philip the Bold commissioned the now near-destroyed Charterhouse of Champmol near Dijon in 1383, it was only natural for him to call in Flemish artists.

Claus Sluter (c. 1345–1406) was one of these. In 1391, he decorated the pediment of this building's portal with a *Virgin and Child* flanked on one side by a statue of the duchess being presented by Saint Catherine and on the other by the duke with Saint John. Over the fountain of the monastery's main cloister, Sluter erected a great crucifixion of which only the hexagonal pediment with its six figures of prophets remains. Viewers are immediately

struck by the monumentality, tragic grandeur and power of Sluter's few surviving works. Their poignancy and strength make them spiritually akin to those done by Michelangelo a century later.

Claus de Werve, Sluter's disciple, continued in the master's footsteps after his death in 1406, completing Philip the Bold's tomb and starting one for John the Fearless. Under a Gothic canopy, forty draped figures march around the bier.

Succeeding John the Fearless in 1420, Philip the Good preferred Flanders to Burgundy and abandoned the work on Champmol. Nevertheless, the influence of Sluter and de Werve spread across Europe,

Tomb of Philippe Pot, Seneschal of Burgundy, attributed to Antoine Le Moiturier. Polychrome stone, between 1477 and 1483. Louvre, Paris. (Photo Giraudon)

and tombs with pallbearers became increasingly popular.

The trend culminated in Burgundy itself in the tomb of Philip the Good's first chamberlain, Philippe Pot (about 1480). The corpse in full armour rests on a slab borne by figures of grieving knights, their features almost hidden by their capes.

The type of Virgin originated by Sluter suffered a less happy fate. Their general lines became increasingly squat and the figures seem lost in a swirl of over-heavy drapery.

Self-portrait, by Nicolas Gerhaert of Leyden. Stone, about 1460. Musée de l'Oeuvre, Strasbourg.

15th CENTURY GERMANY

German burghers benefitted most from the declining power of the Holy Roman Empire. Ways of thinking began to change, and the progress that sculpture had made in the 13th and 14th centuries culminated in a veritable minor renaissance during the 15th.

Strongly affected by the graphic arts, carved drapery no longer followed body lines but, ample and swinging, broke arbitrarily into crisp, dry folds reminiscent of engraving. At the same time, polychrome decoration added to the picturesque effect. Claus Sluter's Flemish-Burgundian style swept the Empire, influencing such sculptors as Nicolas Gerhaert of Leyden (d. 1473), whose over-realistic busts failed to achieve the grandeur of the Master of Dijon. Other exponents of the Flemish-Burgundian style were Hans Multscher (1400–1467) and Jörg Syrlin (c. 1430–1491), who carved the wooden choir stalls of the Ulm cathedral in 1470.

Artists seemed to prefer wood over all other materials, and thus produced a rash of highly intricate altar-pieces. Some famous examples of these were the one at Blaubeuren, partly carved by Gregor Erhart; another at Sankt Wolfgang in Austria, the work of Michael Pacher; and the Issenheim altar-piece sculpted by Nicolas de Haguenau about 1510.

Nuremberg

Weit Stoss (c. 1440–1553), of Nuremberg, the sovereign of woodcarvers, emigrated to Poland, where he sculpted a magnificent polychrome altar-piece for the church of Our Lady in Cracow. Its folding panels bear bas-reliefs showing scenes from the life of Christ, while its main subject, the Assumption and Coronation of the Virgin, is

Station of the Cross, by Adam Krafft. Late 15th century. Germanic Museum, Nuremburg. (Photo Brückmann)

carved in the round. Returning to Nuremberg, Stoss then executed for the church of Saint Lawrence an *Angelic Salutation* which was almost mannerist in its grace.

This unrivalled woodcarver cut deeply into his material and showed a marked taste for sharply broken lines and angular poses. Simultaneously violent and lyrical, his works nevertheless retain a sense of the monumental.

Adam Krafft (c. 1460–1508), a contemporary of Stoss, abandoned wood in favour of stone, which he treated with the same ease and intricacy shown by the woodcarvers of his time. This can be readily seen from his tabernacle for Saint Lawrence in Nuremberg. Krafft's first known work, the *Schreyer Epitaph* on the outside of Saint Sebald in Nuremburg, appears to be an attempt to transmute a painting into sculptural terms. His Stations of the Cross for Nuremberg's Saint John cemetery (Germanic Museum) are calmer and better balanced, showing fewer picture-like traits.

Peter Vischer (c. 1460–c. 1529), another Nuremberger, belonged to the famous Vischer family of bronze casters and foundrymen who supplied baptismal fonts and tombstones for churches throughout Germany. Essentially Gothic in outlook at the start of his career, Vischer, unlike Stoss and Krafft, fell increasingly under Italian influence and his last works clearly show this.

Saint Sebald Reliquary, Nuremburg. Bronze, 1508–1519. A work of Peter Vischer the Elder and his sons in which the Gothic spirit is still evident. (Photo J. P. Viel)

Eve, by Tilmann Riemenschneider. Stone. Nudes like this one play an important part in Riemenschneider's art. Despite the flexibility of the modelling, the pose remains rather stiff. Luitpold Museum, Wurtzburg. (Photo Gundermann)

Würzburg

Although 15th century Nuremberg could claim precedence because of its three great artists, Würzburg too could boast a sculptor of major importance, whose style differed intrinsically from that of his neighbours.

Tilmann Riemenschneider (c. 1460–1531). Set beside Stoss' flair and violence, Riemenschneider's works epitomize calm serenity. For his altarpieces, he rejected polychrome decoration in order to give full value to the carving and, like Vischer, let himself be swayed by the Italians. However, despite the very fine modelling of some of his nude studies, their attitude remains stiff and reveals a sad lack of the anatomical knowledge that contemporary Italian artists had at their fingertips.

14th CENTURY ITALY

Pisa made a strong impact throughout Italy during the late 13th and early 14th centuries, and Giovanni Pisano's pupils came to him from the entire length and breadth of the peninsula.

Tino di Camaino (c. 1285–1337) was one of these. He took his charming talent successively to Siena, Florence and finally Naples and the court of the kings of Anjou. His heavy, solid volumes can be traced back to his early training, but he added a note of Gothic elegance as well, banishing any hint of violence from both expression and movement. On the many tombs he was commissioned to carve, the defunct, enveloped in a weighty shroud, generally adopts a passive, static position.

Like Naples and Milan, Florence too called in Pisan sculptors toward the beginning of the 14th century.

Andrea da Pontedera, better known as **Andrea Pisano** (1270–1349), cast the first bronze doors for Florence's baptistery between 1330 and 1336. His reliefs resemble

Humility, by Andrea Pisano. Bronze, 1330. The baptistery in Florence. To the seven theological and cardinal virtues decorating the door, Pisano added an eighth, Humility. (Photo Giraudon)

150

Giotto's paintings in their open composition and balanced distribution of masses, and show how far Andrea had strayed from the teachings of Giovanni Pisano. Yet the elegance of line and pose in these works is also akin to the French-based international Gothic style which spread over Europe in the wake of miniaturists, ivory carvers and itinerant artists.

Andrea's grace and elegance came to flower in the works of his son, Nino, who specialized in serenely smiling Madonnas.

Andrea di Cione, known as **Orcagna** (active from 1344 to 1368) was simultaneously a painter, sculptor, architect and goldsmith, thus foreshadowing the humanist geniuses of the Quattrocento. The supreme example of his art is the monumental gold tabernacle for Saint Michele in Florence (1349–1359), decorated with bas-relief scenes from the Virgin's life.

Thus by the end of the 14th century, the two trends which were to flourish in Quattrocento Florence had already appeared: the tragic sense of human destiny prevalent in the works of Giovanni Pisano, and the delight in pure formal beauty reflected in Andrea Pisano's sculpture.

Madonna and Child, by Nino Pisano. Late 14th century. Santa Maria della Spina, Pisa. The vigorous organization of the drapery and general sobriety of the whole are notable. (Photo Giraudon)

14th and 15th CENTURIES IN SPAIN

Spanish Gothic sculpture of the 14th century was initially strongly marked by the French style before gradually falling under the sway of Flemish and then Italian influences. In Pamplona, for instance, the French Bishop, Arnaud de Barbezan, called in a Frenchman, Jacques Perrut, to decorate his cloister.

Flemish influence reigned throughout the 15th century and Janin Lomme of Tournai was commissioned to sculpt the tomb of Charles III the Noble and his queen, Eleanor in Pamplona (1416).

Saint Thecla altar-piece, detail, by Johann de Vallfogona. About 1426–1450. Tarragona Cathedral. (Photo Boudot-Lamotte)

Flemish and German artists encouraged local woodcarving so that large polychrome altar-pieces covered with pictorial scenes soon became the rage, particularly in Catalonia. The famous Saint Thecla altar-piece in Tarragona's cathedral, the work of Johann de Vallfogona (1426–1450), is typically Flemish.

The plateresque style in architecture with its rich orna-

Tomb of Juan de Padilla, by Gil de Siloé. Stone. The simplicity of the pose and flexible modelling reflect Italian influence. Burgos Museum. (Photo Ségalat)

mentation also had serious repercussions on altar-pieces carved during the last half of the 15th century. This can be seen from the works of the period's finest sculptor, Gil de Siloé (a native of Antwerp who lived in Burgos from 1486 onward). The details incorporated into his altar-piece for the Charterhouse of Miraflores (1496–1499) are overwhelmingly rich. The wood is twisted and undercut, with decorative details enmeshed in the reliefs so that not a pinpoint of space remains barren. A similar insistence on cluttered opulence can be seen in the niche and frame of the Infanta Alfonso's tomb at Miraflores, as well as in the clothing of Juan de Padilla's funerary statue now in the Burgos Museum. But the simplicity of attitude and suppleness of modelling in this work clearly reveal the influence of the Italian Quattrocento in Spain.

By the end of the 15th century, Spanish sculpture finally managed to relax a bit and free itself from the graphic realism imported from Flanders.

12th to 15th CENTURIES IN PORTUGAL

From the 12th to the 15th century, Portugal, like Spain, remained under the sway of French art, thanks partly to help from the great monastic orders of Templars and Cistercians in wresting the kingdom back from the Moors.

The Cistercian abbey of Alcobaça, founded in 1153, contains two magnificent tombs in the French style. Carved for Pedro I and Ines de Castro, the "Dead Queen," they rank high among 14th century recumbent figures.

Flemish influence also infiltrated Portugal as woodcarvers came from Flanders to decorate many Portuguese churches with altar screens and choir stalls.

In the Manueline style that developed during the reign of Manuel the Great (1495–1521), Gothic structures were covered with exuberant, deeply carved motifs in which marine flora and fauna and navigational instruments recalled Portugal's momentous overseas discoveries. The style's overall pattern and interlocking designs, as well as an almost total absence of human figures, shows its close kinship to Arabic art. Portuguese sculpture was prevented from becoming entirely ornamental by the arrival of French and Spanish sculptors at the start of the 16th century.

Window from the Templars' church in Tomar, attributed to Diogo de Arruda. Stone, late 15th century. Its over-elaborate decoration with maritime overtones is typical of Manueline art. (Photo Boudot-Lamotte)

12th TO 15th CENTURIES IN ENGLAND

At a time when Gothic Europe's churches and cathedrals seemed positively to burgeon with statuary, sculpture played only a minor role in England, appearing only in the form of the charming, often luxuriant foliage used to point up an architectural line.

British sculpture during the 13th and 14th centuries in many ways resembled its French counterpart, though a note of originality appeared in the elaborately carved tombs placed in or near sanctuaries. In contrast to French practice, subjects were usually portrayed alive in action.

British sculpture would have no part of the realism prevalent on the continent during the 15th century, and the result was a rather forbidding, extreme sobriety, not to say stiffness and aridity. Funerary art was limited to bronze recumbent figures or simple, engraved brass plates set in church floors.

Alabaster sculpture also became popular at this time, particularly in the Nottingham area, and small alabaster carvings from England flowed onto foreign markets, either in the form of panels to be inlaid or as portable altarpieces. Gilding and polychrome paint were used to relieve the monotony of the carving.

The Black Prince, bronze recumbent figure, about 1377–1380. Canterbury Cathedral. This figure was strongly influenced by contemporary French works. (Photo Boudot-Lamotte)

from the renaissance
to contemporary
times |

5

The humanistic Renaissance which began to spread over Italy at the start of the 14th century was not simply the offshoot of a vogue for antiquity but represented an entirely different conception of the universe. Whereas the medieval world was essentially God-inspired, the Renaissance concentrated on man. "First nature displaced God as the goal of art, then God was unseated by the human intelligence as art's source." (L. Venturi).

Chained Slave, by Michelangelo. Marble, 1513–1514. One of two captives carved for the sculptor's original design for Pope Julius II's tomb. Louvre, Paris. (Photo Giraudon)

Henceforth, artists suddenly aware of their own originality broke away from the humble anonymity imposed during the construction of the great cathedrals. Art for art's sake developed as a cult. Besides this new-found individuality, aesthetic and intellectual factors, as well as contemporary scientific discoveries, all had a profound impact on artistic development. As sculpture freed itself from its architectural framework, portrait busts appeared and gardens bloomed with statues, many celebrating the beauties of the nude human body. Although remaining true to nature and inspired by the great Greco-Roman sculptural traditions, artists yet managed to express themselves.

15th AND 16th CENTURIES IN ITALY

15th century Florence

The 15th century, an unrivalled period of economic, cultural and artistic glory in Florence, opened with one of the most momentous events in the entire history of sculpture—a competition for the second door of the baptistery (1401). Several artists presented their versions of the chosen subject—the sacrifice of Isaac. Filippo Brunelleschi (1377–1446), Lorenzo Ghiberti (1378–1455) and Jacopo della Quercia (c. 1374–1438) all were in the running, but finally the jury favoured Ghiberti's balanced composition and elegantly refined, yet slightly Gothic style over Brunelleschi's violence and daring use of perspective.

Ghiberti spent over twenty years, from 1403 to 1424, executing twenty-eight quadrilobed bronze panels depicting scenes from the life of Christ to match the design of older doors sculpted by Andrea Pisano. Later Ghiberti received the commission for still a third set of baptistery doors and between 1425 and 1452 executed sixteen large bronze

The Sacrifice of Isaac, competition pieces for the second door of Florence's baptistery. Gilded bronze, 1401. Left, Filippo Brunelleschi's version; right, that of Lorenzo Ghiberti. (Photo Alinari-Giraudon)

panels showing Old Testament scenes. Admiring the flawless technique, rich composition and plastic effects of these pictorial bas-reliefs, Michelangelo dubbed them "The Gates of Paradise."

Whereas Ghiberti's refined art paid homage to Gothic traditions, his contemporaries, Nanni di Banco and Jacopo della Quercia, looked further back to antique models and laid more stress on the human figure.

Nanni di Banco (c. 1380–1421) carved the *Four Crowned Saints* (about 1410) whose flowing togas and stern faces clearly derive from Roman senators. However, the niches in which they are displayed on the walls of the church of Orsanmichele are unmistakably Gothic.

Tomb of Illaria del Carretto, by Jacopo della Quercia. Marble, 1407. Lucca Cathedral. (Photó Giraudon)

Siena

Jacopo della Quercia (c. 1374–1438), a native of Siena, carved a magnificent tomb for Illaria del Carretto in the cathedral of Lucca. Here, a recumbent figure half hidden in its shroud is essentially medieval, while the sarcophagus with its simple garlands, flowers and cupids almost duplicates an antique model. The same power of execution and simplicity of line may be found in the vigorously styled bas-reliefs, reminiscent of Donatello, that he executed for Siena's *Fonte Gaia* (1409–1419).

159

Equestrian statue of the **Condottiere Gattamelata,** by Donatello. Bronze, 1447. Padua. (Photo Anderson-Giraudon)

Donatello

Donatello (1386–1466), who studied with Ghiberti and worked with Brunelleschi, unquestionably ranks as the master sculptor of Florence's Quattrocento. Whether working in rough stone, marble or bronze, he had dazzling technique, and his daring sculptural innovations in relief work as well as free-standing figures made him a truly revolutionary artist. Concentrating on the human figure and scorning conventions of pose, drapery and expression, Donatello produced powerfully realistic figures.

One of his earlier works, the *Saint George* carved for the church of Orsanmichele in 1416 (Bargello Museum, Florence), represents a fully armed young knight, who, still slightly off balance according to the Gothic canon, bristles with energy. Donatello used the same inherent drama and realistic treatment in the two prophets carved for Florence's Duomo between 1423 and 1436: *Jeremiah* and *Habakkuk*— or Zuccone as he is known locally because of his gourd-like head.

Donatello renewed his acquaintance with antique

statuary during a trip to Rome about 1432–33, but on returning to Florence persisted in introducing a dramatic and violent note into otherwise classical works. Typical are his *cantorie*, or frieze of singers, for the cathedral, whose lightly draped cherubs lead a mad, bacchanalian dance.

In 1443 Donatello moved to Padua where he remained for nearly ten years. Several of his major works were executed there, including the altar of the Basilica del Santo and the celebrated *Gattamelata*, the first equestrian bronze to be cast since Roman days. Donatello's presence in Padua inspired a whole new school of sculptors in that city, best represented by Niccolo Pizzolo.

The essential tragedy of life so often glimpsed in Donatello's works became even more visible after his return to Florence as can be seen in the baptistery's dramatic, almost fleshless *Mary Magdalene*. Her skeleton-like body vividly contrasts with the lithe adolescence of his early

Young musicians, detail from a cantoria in the Duomo, Florence, by Donatello. Marble, 1433. (Photo Alinari-Giraudon)

bronze *David*. Donatello's last works were an unfinished series of bas-reliefs decorating the pulpits of Florence's church of San Lorenzo. Every kind of geometric and optical perspective can be seen in these remarkable reliefs, for Donatello made free use of architectural forms, arranged his figures in the most unconventional manner and even employed the *schiacciato* technique, in which solid forms are suggested by the shallowest relief.

Donatello's influence

Though Donatello's influence continued throughout the Quattrocento, it was understandably most strongly felt by his contemporaries.

Lucca della Robbia (1400–1482), a goldsmith by training, spent the years between 1431 and 1438 carving a companion piece for Donatello's *cantorie* but in an entirely different idiom. In contrast to the frenetic violence of the latter's singers, della Robbia's discreetly realistic choirboys epitomize well-behaved serenity. The technique that Lucca della Robbia invented allowed him to make the most of his penchant for gracefully flowing curves, and many of his works are executed in a highly glazed terra-cotta in which light blues, whites and yellows predominate. Rapidly popular because of its inherent elegance and delicacy, this technique was also employed by the artists's numerous descendants. The medallions of infants wrapped in swaddling clothes, with which

Young singers, detail from a cantoria in the Duomo, Florence, by Lucca della Robbia. Marble, 1431–1438. (Photo Anderson-Giraudon).

Diana on Her Chariot, detail from the decoration of the Malatesta Temple, Rimini, by Agostino di Duccio. Marble, about 1450. (Photo Scala)

della Robbia decorated Brunelleschi's home for foundlings (Innocenti) in Florence, were also of this material.

Many sculptors were inspired by Donatello's great works.

Agostino di Duccio (1418–1481), one of these, composed for Rimini's Malatesta Tempietto a vast allegory crowded with entwined *putti* (cherubs) clad in swirling drapery.

Desiderio da Settignano (1428–1464) was far more realistic in his approach and had a rigorous sense of structure which made him Donatello's star pupil and apostle.

In the first half of the 15th century, portrait busts and funerary monuments became popular in Italy, the finest example of the latter being the tomb of Leonardo Bruni in Florence's Santa Croce church executed by Bernardo Rossellino in 1444. A student of the architect Alberti, he applied classical motifs to the staggered forms of Gothic tombs, thus creating a type of funerary monument which was to be long imitated.

local schools

By 1460–1470, the seeds sown by the Florentine masters had reached every corner of Italy, and Florence could not maintain unrivalled leadership. Gradually local schools of sculpture arose here and there. One of Donatello's students, Bartolomeo Bellano (c. 1434–1492) set up shop in Padua, while in Venice Antonio Rizzo (c. 1430–

1499) exhibited a sure sense of volume and a talent for delicate modelling, and Pietro Lombardo (1435–1515) revealed a detail and excessively fine execution which anticipated mannerism. In Urbino, the ducal palace of the Montefeltro family was decorated in the Florentine manner of sculpture by the Tuscan Domenico Rosselli (c. 1439–1497). The Dalmatian Francesco Laurana (c. 1420–1503) also worked for the local dukes before moving on to France and then Naples. The rigorous simplicity and stylization of his female portrait busts prove the vast influence exercised by the painter Piero della Francesca at the Montefeltro court.

The works of the Bolognese master Niccolo Dell'Arca (1440–1494) diametrically opposed Florentine precepts in their dramatic expressionism, and the same can be said of statues by Guido Mazzoni (1450–1518) of Modena. A similar defiance of Florentine domination can be seen in the art of Lombardy, where an offshoot of the international Gothic style held sway throughout the 15th century. Here materials are roughly chiselled to create dramatic effects, folds break sharply and decorative elements tend to be heavy and close-set.

Bust of Eleanor of Aragon, by Francesco Laurana. Marble, about 1467–1471. Its simplicity and purity are typical of Laurana's works. Louvre, Paris. (Photo Scala)

16th century Florence

Idealistic humanism seemed to govern Florence after Donatello's death. Sculptors were in great demand and flourished, basking in the protection of such wealthy patrons as the Medicis. Florentine art had reached a dazzling peak of perfection and luxury beyond which it seemed impossible to rise, and the foremost artists of the day were Pollaiuolo and Verrocchio.

Antonio del Pollaiolo (1432–1498) was simultaneously painter and sculptor, and his statue of *Hercules Crushing Anteus* (Bargello Museum) beautifully renders muscular tension and powerful realism, despite the angular aridity of its contours. Pollaiuolo's way with bronze can best be seen in his tomb for Sixtus IV, in Saint Peter's in Rome.

Its strikingly original composition—a simple elevated slab adorned with leaves and allegorical figures—plus the vigorous, full style employed, gives it unaffected nobility.

Andrea di Cione, known as **Verrocchio** (1435–1488), a painter, goldsmith, and sculptor, patronized by the Medicis, often followed Donatello in his choice of subjects (David, equestrian statues, *putti*).

Tomb of Sixtus IV, by Antonio Pollaiolo. The sculptor's mastery of bronze shows in the casting of this magnificent tomb. Saint Peter's, Rome. (Photo Alinari-Giraudon)

He treated them, however, with an exaggerated sensitivity and psychological insight that somewhat diminished the strength and significance of the theme. But the fact that Verrocchio could also banish all superfluous artifice is fully attested to in his monument to the Medicis (1472, church of San Lorenzo, Florence). This work consists of a simple sarcophagus with heavy bronze legs etched with acanthus leaves.

MICHELANGELO

Michelangelo Buonarroti (1475–1564), western civilization's artist supreme since the decline of the ancient world, was born in Florence just nine years after Donatello's death, and as the living symbol of the Renaissance, this profoundly humanistic genius anticipated our contemporary concern with art's spiritual values. "He was so concerned with the tragedy of human destiny

Tomb of Giacomo and Pietro de Medici, by Verrocchio. Marble and bronze, 1472. Church of San Lorenzo, Florence. (Photo Alinari-Giraudon)

that he saw no other purpose in art than to use the human figure to show the variety of mankind's passions and their sublimation in faith. To him, sculpture was the highest form of art, enabling, as it did, latent forms in materials to be freed by the artist's intuition" (A. Chastel).

Michelangelo showed his sovereign talent in turn as poet, architect, painter, sculptor and goldsmith, and he excelled in all of these fields. After his studies in the painter Ghirlandaio's Florentine studio, he carefully studied the works of Donatello and the few antique remains to be found in his native Florence. Forced into exile by political upheavals, he took refuge in Rome, where he executed the famous *Pietà* now in Saint Peter's. The drapery and flexible poses of his figures

Pietà, by Michelangelo, executed as a young man during his first visit to Rome. Marble, 1498–1501. Saint Peter's, Rome. (Photo J. Roubier)

David, detail. Marble, 1501–1503. Michelangelo here expresses his dream of heroic humanity. Accademia, Florence. (Photo Anderson-Giraudon)

testify to his fine early technique as well as his thorough knowledge of anatomy. The incomparable marble *David* which he carved with such bold strokes on his return to Florence in 1501 further demonstrated his heroic vision of humanity.

In 1505, Michelangelo was summoned to Rome by Pope Julius II to carve his tomb and paint the ceiling of the Sistine Chapel. Although he provided several designs for the tomb and worked on it throughout most of his life (1505–1545), it was never completed. The part that can now be seen in the church of San Pietro in Vincoli (Rome) bears no resemblance whatever to Michelangelo's original project, which called for a four-stage pyramid of which the last was to be the Pope's sarcophagus. As it now stands, only the facades of two stages are complete, with the statues of Faith, Charity, and Moses; the triumphal spirit of Michelangelo's original concept is entirely lost.

Back in Florence between 1520 and 1534, the prodigious artist worked on the facing tombs of Dukes Giuliano and Lorenzo Medici in a chapel of the church of San Lorenzo. The two dukes sit enthroned above their sarcophagi, on which are two reclining figures, *Night* and *Day* for the tomb of Giuliano and *Dawn* and *Dusk* for Lorenzo. In these figures, Michelangelo established a contrast between smoothly polished and carefully modelled areas and the remaining merely sketched-in parts. In addition to this blithe freedom of execution, he intentionally distorted and elongated natural forms for purely aesthetic purposes.

Returning to Rome (1534–1564), Michelangelo was commissioned by Pope Paul II to paint the fabulous fresco of the *Last Judgement* for the Sistine Chapel and to act as architect for Saint Peter's, thus leaving him scant time for sculpture. His last works were three *Pietàs* (cathedral of Florence, the Accademia, Florence, and Milan Museum), including the unfinished *Rondanini Pietà*. In all of his sculpture, muscular and psychological tension convey a desperate anxiety and pain which movingly express the human condition.

Twilight, detail from Lorenzo de Medici's tomb, by Michelangelo. Marble, 1524–1533. Church of San Lorenzo, Florence. (Photo Anderson-Giraudon)

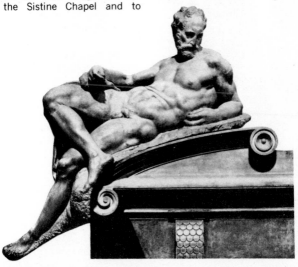

the disciples

Except for Andrea Contucci, better known as Sansovino (1460–1529), who attempted to transpose Leonardo's delicate style into sculpture, most of Michelangelo's followers were dwarfed by their mentor's towering stature. Among these Cinquecento (16th century) artists we might mention Baccio Bandinelli (1493–1560), Giovanni Francesco Rusticci (1474–1554), Giovanni Angelo Da Montorsoli (d. 1563), and Tribolo (1500–1550). Sadly, these proselytes ignored the tragic and heroic meaning of their preceptor's works. Instead, they concentrated on decorative values and elegance of line.

In Venice, however, Alessandro Vittoria (1525–1608) and Jacopo Tatti (1486–1570), who was also called Sansovino, established a new sculptural tradition. In this they combined Michelangelo's strength and vigorous style with an elegant, symmetrical, classical approach which avoided mannerism's excessive refinements.

The Rondanini Pietà. Started in Michelangelo's last year of life, it was never finished. Milan Museum. (Photo Giraudon)

mannerism

Just after Michelangelo's death, an artistic trend developed in Florence whose basic elements had already been supplied by the master. This movement consisted of a search for an elegant, idealized style and a refined and subtle "manner." Mannerist sculptors went in for pure, free-flowing lines and poses, flaunting their virtuosity in composition and frequently abandoning the monumental in favour of smaller, more intimate works. This trend explains how Florence and Padua soon became producers of statuettes and bronze medallions. This type of sculpture, popular with collectors, was practiced by many excellent artists, of whom the most celebrated was Andrea Riccio (1470–1552).

Benvenuto Cellini (1500–1571), goldsmith and sculptor in bronze, looms as one of Florence's fabulous 16th century artists, and in the course of his romantic life spent some time in France

Perseus, by Benvenuto Cellini. Bronze, 1553. The goldsmith's exquisite virtuosity is amply displayed in his treatment of anatomical details and decorative elements. Loggia dei Lanzi, Florence. (Photo Ségalat)

Mercury Flying, by Giambologna. Bronze, 1564. National Museum, Florence. (Photo Alinari-Giraudon)

working for Francis I. His incredible inventiveness and sometimes preposterously precious elegance at times resulted in such oddities as the famous gold salt-cellar made for Francis I, now in the Vienna Museum. His virtuosity occasionally even hampered his expressive strength, as in the case of *Perseus Holding the Head of Medusa,* now in the Loggia dei Lanzi, Florence.

Giambologna, or **Jean de Bologne** (1529–1608), who trained under Jacques Debroecq in Antwerp, modified and refined a taste for opulence acquired during his Flemish apprenticeship when, exposed to classicism, he fell under the spell of the Italian Renaissance. Settling in Florence, he soon adopted the elegant forms and poses of Cellini's elongated figures. In some cases, the rhythmical body movements and carefully studied balance of his figures appear as cleverness and nothing more. Giambologna's workshop did much to spread mannerist doctrines throughout Europe.

16th CENTURY FRANCE

The links between Italy and France which had been forged back in the Middle Ages became even stronger toward the end of the 15th century, due to the wars arising from France's claim to the kingdom of Naples and the duchy of Milan.

Italian influence

The French who accompanied Charles VIII on his first expedition over the Alps were immediately dazzled by Italian art, and so brought back several artists with them. These included Girolamo da Fiesole, Guido Mazzoni and the brothers Giusti. During this first renaissance, which covered the reigns of Charles VIII (1483–1498) and Louis XII (1498–1515), Italian traditions slowly insinuated themselves into French art, mainly as decorative motifs.

That supreme patron of "Italian style" art, the archbishop of Rouen, Georges d'Amboise, employed Italian artists to decorate his residence at Gaillon, as well as the French

Saint George and the Dragon, altar-piece executed by Michel Colombe for the chapel of Cardinal d'Amboise's Château de Gaillon. Marble, early 16th century. (Photo Ségalat)

sculptor Michel Colombe (1430–1515), who rather late in life had adopted the transalpine style. Colombe's colleagues quickly followed his lead and a school centred in Touraine soon started turning out serious, elegant and floatingly draped statues.

A similar phenomenon occurred in Champagne, where the "Saint Martha" school of Troyes produced works which combined Gothic modesty with the ease and grace of contemporary Italian statues. Sculpture in the Italian manner by French artists flowed to vast castles being built by the feudal lords of France.

Returning from captivity after the battle of Pavia (1526), Francis I summoned many Italian artists to his court. They included Rosso, who came to France in 1530, Primaticcio (1532), Rusticci (1527), and even Cellini. Rosso and then Primaticcio exercised almost dictatorial power over French artists and quickly spread the brilliant bloom of the mannerist school over all France.

Saint Martha, French school of 16th century. Painted stone. Italian grace joins Gothic sobriety in this piece from the workshops of Troyes. Church of la Madeleine, Troyes. (Photo J. P. Vieil)

Bas-relief from the Fountain of the Innocents, Paris, by Jean Goujon. Stone, 1549. (Photo DCO)

the classical renaissance

During the reign of Henry II (1519–1559), French sculptors participated in the current wave of humanism and, following their Italian masters, sought inspiration in antiquity.

Jean Goujon (c. 1510–1566) spent a large part of his life collaborating with the architect Pierre Lescot. In 1549 he executed the exquisite bas-reliefs on the Fountain of the Innocents in Paris. Despite the stretched-out forms of these figures, inspired by Rosso and Primaticcio, Goujon managed to combine whirling forms in body and drapery with a purity more akin to classical Greece. His reverence for antiquity is even more transparent in the caryatids he carved for the Louvre, which are close cousins to those of the Erechtheum on the Athenian Acropolis. He ended his days an exile in Bologna.

Pierre Bontemps (1507–1570), who was stylistically more vigorous than his contemporary Jean Goujon, concentrated on anecdotal qualities. His works are all discreetly realistic and undeniably influenced by the Italian mannerists.

175

Germain Pilon (1537–1590). Upon Henry II's death in 1559, Primaticcio was named superintendent of buildings. To execute a funeral monument for the Valois kings, commissioned for the basilica of Saint Denis by Catherine de Medici, he chose a young sculptor called Germain Pilon, noted for the incomparable technique of his portraits. The gripping realism of Pilon's works never overshadowed their elegance and expressiveness. Nevertheless, his later works, such as the *Virgin of Pity* and *Saint Francis*, show how his style evolved. Their sensitivity and the expression of violent emotions

Saint Francis in Ecstasy, by Germain Pilon, 1580. A fine example of this artist's tendency to realism. Church of Saint Jean and Saint Francis, Paris. (Photo Giraudon)

anticipate the baroque tendencies that Bernini displayed some fifty years later.

Pilon's sculpture, like that of Goujon and Bontemps, was quite innocent of the Italian influence, which had served only as a catalyst in French art. Pilon thus appears more as a link between a relaxed form of Gothic realism and the moderate baroque which appeared toward the end of Henry IV's reign.

16th CENTURY SPAIN

Spain's power reached its peak during the 16th century, when Florentine sculptors were mainly responsible for introducing Renaissance art into that country. Queen Isabella imported Domenico Fancelli (1469–1519) to carve the tomb of the Infanta Don Juan in the church of San Tomas in Avila (completed in 1512). Pietro Torrigianni (1472–1528), a colleague of Michelangelo, had to flee Florence and after a spell in England, moved on to Charles V's court in Spain. His works, many of them in painted terra-cotta, show a careful execution and stark realism.

Santo Domingo de la Calzada altar-piece, by Damian Forment. Wood, 1538. (Photo J. P. Vieil)

Italian influence

Two contemporary Spanish artists strongly influenced by these Italians were Vasco de la Zarza (d. 1524), who skillfully applied the lessons learned from his Florentine masters, and Bartoloméo Ordóñez (d. 1520), who trained for many years in Italy, returned to Barcelona and then went back to work in his adopted country. To him we owe chiefly the tombs of King Philip I the Handsome and Queen Juana the Mad at Granada.

Aragon's leading sculptor was Damian Forment (d. 1543), a specialist in large altar-pieces. Lombard and classical tendencies can be seen in his work, particularly in the wooden alabaster-based altar-piece carved for the church of Santo Domingo de la Calzada in 1538.

Alonso Berruguete (1490–1561), the greatest Spanish sculptor to appear during the opulent reign of Charles V, trained under Michelangelo. But the extreme realism of his funerary monuments and the mass of decorative elements he favoured make his works a far cry from those of the master. He also abandoned the marble so dear to Italians in order to work in wood, in which he sculpted contorted figures and on which he often painted. It was in wood that he executed one of his masterpieces—the choir stalls for Toledo's cathedral (1539–1548).

About this time several French and Flemish sculptors also came to Spain, among them Philippe Biguerny and Jean de Juny. In the violence of their movement, de Juny's works seem more typical of Spanish art than those produced by native artists. Among his many statues are the *Entombed Christ* (Valladolid Museum) and the *Dead Christ* (Segovia Cathedral).

The reign of Phillip II (1556–1598) was marked by the preponderance of Italian over Spanish artists. In austere style, Leone Leoni and his son Pompeo (c. 1533–1608) cast the monumental bronzes which decorate the altar screen and tombs of the church of the Escorial, and the impressive royal tombs of Charles V and Phillip II.

An Apostle, by Philippe Oudart. Terra-cotta, 16th century. Oudart was the most individualistic and realistic of the French artists working in Portugal. Beaux Arts Museum, Coimbra. (Photo Boudot-Lamotte)

16th CENTURY PORTUGAL

French artists were mainly responsible for bringing the Renaissance to Portugal, and the fantasies of Portuguese sculptors were consequently progressively replaced by the newest fashions that developed in Italian art.

Nicolas Chantereine (first mentioned in 1517) spent many years decorating the churches of Santa Croce and Sé Velha in Coimbra in the Italian style, before directing work on the main door of the Belém monastery in Lisbon.

Jean de Rouen established himself in Coimbra in 1530 and produced numerous altar screens and bas-reliefs in the Italian style. Arriving in the same year, Philippe Oudart showed a trenchant individuality in monumental sculpture. Nevertheless, his realistic art did not seem to exert the same influence as that of his compatriots.

16th CENTURY IN THE LOW COUNTRIES

By the 16th century, the Netherlands also were touched by the Italian contagion sweeping Europe. Oddly enough, one vital centre of this Flemish Renaissance was in France at Brou, where Marguerite of Austria (1480–1530), who had become regent of the Netherlands in 1506, decided to build tombs for her family. In 1516 she called upon the Flemish sculptor Jean de Bruxelles, who in turn was replaced by a German, Conrad Meyt (or Conrad de Malines) in 1526. Structurally these tombs are in the Gothic manner; Italian influence shows in the decoration and recumbent figures.

Similar new decorative elements also appeared in the

Franc chimney. Stone, 1538. The work of several sculptors, it combines Italian with Flemish-Gothic influences. Bruges. (Photo J. P. Vieil)

great Flemish altar-pieces. Antique-style pilasters replaced Gothic pillars, and garlands superseded tufts of foliage. Such Italian elements are particularly noticeable in the bas-relief of Susannah and the Elders over the monumental chimney of the court clerk's office in Bruges, executed by Guyot de Beaugrand and his co-workers between 1528 and 1532.

Still another example of Italiana is the handsome alabaster altar-piece which Jean Monne (d. c. 1548) made for Saint Martin de Hal in 1533.

Jacques Dubroecq (c. 1500–1584), a native of Mons, went to Italy where he immediately fell under the spell of Michelangelo. His *Virtue* for Sainte Wandru in Mons illustrates his flexible approach to monumental pieces. For the decade from 1544 to 1554 Giambologna trained in Dubroecq's studio.

Corneille de Vriendt, known as **Floris** (1514–1575), a tremendously prolific artist, enthusiastically adopted in Flanders the Italian fad for grotesques. His extraordinary tabernacle in Léau (1550–1552) shows how he blended transalpine elements into the Gothic tradition.

Mannerist influence predominated in Flanders from 1560–1570 onward. Many sculptors, including Alexander Colin, Hubert Gerhardt and Adrien de Vries moved eastward to the Hapsburg court where they proved to be the most fervent disciples of the new Italian school.

Decoration of Antwerp City Hall, by Corneille Floris, 1561–1565. On his return from Italy, Floris popularized Italian decorative techniques in Flanders. (Photo J. P. Vieil)

16th CENTURY
IN THE GERMANIC COUNTRIES

Germany's artistic flowering during the 15th century was followed in the 16th century by a simmering down of activity due to religious and political strife. Nevertheless, the second half of that century was strongly marked by the imprint of Italian mannerism.

While Peter Vischer's bronze reliquary for Saint Sebald in Nuremberg remained fundamentally Gothic in outlook, certain details of its base and the lower part of the pillars show a definite Italian influence. This trend showed itself even more strongly in the two magnificent statues Vischer executed for the tomb of Emperor Maximilian in Innsbruck's Franciscan church; their elegant poses are a far cry from the "Gothic S" of former times.

The Vischer studio, which also worked for the Fugger family, Augsburg's leading bankers and patrons of the arts, provided that city with some of its outstanding monuments. Hubert Gerhardt (c. 1540–1630) was responsible for the Fountain of Augustus, while Adrien de Vries executed both the Fountain of Mercury and the Fountain of Hercules.

Italian Renaissance styles traveled also to the court in Vienna, as Emperor Maximilian II (1527–1576) summoned artists from far and wide. All seem to have adopted the tenets of mannerism as elaborated in Giambologna's Florentine studio. Among these were Wenzel Jamnitzer (1508–1585), Gerhardt and Alexander Colin (1527–1612) —later to be known as "the Flemish Ghiberti."

On the death of Emperor Maximilian, his son Rudolph II (1552–1612) continued to encourage in Prague the refined worldly art of the international mannerist school led by Adrien de Vries, a Flemish sculptor who had himself studied under Giambologna.

In Munich the elector of Bavaria, Maximilian (1573–1651), also used the talent of sculptors, such as Gerhardt, skilled in Italian-style ornamentation.

Spring, by Wenzel Jamnitzer. Gilded copper, about 1557. The mannerist influence clearly seen here was also evident in the other three statues once supporting a fountain of the seasons. (Photo Boudot-Lamotte)

Fountain of Mercury, Augsburg, by Adrien de Vries. Bronze, late 16th century. Italian mannerism was strongly felt in this sculptor's works. (Photo J. P. Vieil)

Tomb of Cardinal de Berulle, by Jacques Sarrazin. Marble, 1657. Sarrazin's measured style is already quite classical. Louvre, Paris. (Photo Verrouts)

17th CENTURY FRANCE

From 1590, there developed in France a new concept of classical beauty, with the result that the country gradually detached itself from Italian influences.

classicism

Jacques Sarrazin (1588–1660), who had spent the eighteen years between 1610 and 1628 in Italy, led the new school of French sculpture on his return to Paris. Although exposed in Rome to contemporary Italian baroque as well as the splendours of ancient masterpieces, Sarrazin subsequently abandoned all baroque influence and was instrumental in establishing the classical cannon. His works show a calm and balanced execution in which emotion reveals itself only through a tempered realism.

Sarrazin's numerous gifted pupils included Gilles Guérin, Gerard Van Obstal, Lerambert, the brothers Marsy, and Pierre Legros. All these worked together at Versailles, along with many bronze workers and medallists such as Jean Varin, Guillaume Dupré, Nicolas Guillain and his son Simon. By the austerity of its execution, young Guillain's *Pont du Change Monument*

(1647, now in the Louvre) modified traditional French realism once and for all.

The brothers **Anguier, François** (1604–1669) and **Michel** (1612–1686) skilfully used the lessons of antiquity and the polished techniques they had learned from Algardi in Rome. Both worked under the master designers of Versailles: Le Vau, Le Brun and Le Nôtre. Michel was responsible for the exquisite *Amphitrite* (Louvre), which once graced the Ladies' Grove in the park of Versailles.

On Sarrazin's initiative, and probably with Le Brun's encouragement, a new academy was formed in 1648 destined

The Rhone, by J. B. Tuby. Bronze, 1687–1690. Eight statues representing the rivers of France decorate the basins in front of Versailles. (Photo Giraudon)

to liberate artists from the rigid controls of the establishment and the cut-and-dried laws of their crafts. Sponsored by Louis XIV, the Royal Academy of Painting and Sculpture received its first charter in 1665. Its foundation is especially important as, having become the docile instrument of the superintendent of fine arts, it eventually led to a general standardization in artistic thought and resulted, especially in the 17th century, in the establishment of an official school of sculpture.

official art

Securely ensconced on the throne and diligently supported by a coterie of servile ministers, Louis XIV felt the need for an official art form—a style to be based on antiquity, and whose sole purpose was to glorify the Sun King and his works. Bernini's trip to France to champion Italian baroque proved a failure, partly because of ministerial plots but also because the king himself developed a deep antipathy to this violent form of art.

Louis XIV did, however, provide his artists with a wonder project—the construction of Versailles with its magnificent park and gardens. Work began in 1663 and continued in spite of financial difficulties until the end of his reign in

Bust of Louis XIV, by Jean Varin. Marble, 1665. The medallist's fine art is displayed in this statue. Versailles Museum. (Photo Giraudon)

1715. The vast possibilities thus offered by the king were gratefully accepted by a group of sculptors working under the direction of Charles Le Brun (until his death in 1690 and thereafter under Jules Hardouin-Mansart). Le Brun provided the original designs, which the sculptors executed more or less faithfully. The symbolism behind some of these works was extremely abstruse and complicated; their subjects were derived mainly from antiquity.

Girardon and Coysevox proved outstanding among this group.

François Girardon (1628–1715), as an artist, was both pliant and subtle. An admirer of antiquity and a superb technician, he maintained the tradition of elegance, flexibility and grace initiated by Jean Goujon. In the bas-relief *Nymphs Bathing* at Versailles, as well as in *Winter* in the palace's gardens, a friendly yet refined art shines through the outwardly stiff mask of classicism.

Antoine Coysevox (1640–1720) was the first and foremost sculptor of Louis XIV. In executing antique copies for the gardens of Versailles (the Louvre's *Kneeling Venus* is typical), he was nonetheless able to get far enough

Winter, by François Girardon. Marble, 1680. The most celebrated of the four seasons commissioned by the statesman Colbert for the gardens at Versailles. (Photo Giraudon)

away from the model to create an original work of art. Busts executed by this artist are also significant. His masterpiece is undoubtedly the bronze bust of the *Great Condé* (Prince Louis II), now in the Louvre. Here, with spare economy and no dramatics, he brought out the sharp intelligence and somewhat irascible character of his subject.

187

Puget and baroque art

Quite apart from the official art, which was classical, a baroque tendency began to appear in France during the 17th and 18th centuries.

Pierre Puget (1620–1694) of Marseilles headed this wave. Back in his native country after a prolonged stay in Italy, Puget sought royal commissions and executed both his colossal bas-relief, *Alexander and Diogenes*, and his famed *Milo of Crotone* for Versailles. Yet barely had these works been installed in the royal residence than they were rejected—another setback for baroque. The fact is that the sense of tragedy Puget had tried to express, and even the sense of painful struggle, ran counter to the academic doctrines of the day. Toward the end of Louis' reign, and especially after Le Brun, this academic outlook softened somewhat. Sculptors were allowed more freedom to express motion (though not of course violence), and a certain grace and elegance began to be seen in some statues. Typical of this transitional interim was Coysevox's ravishing portrait of Duchess Adelaide of Burgundy as *Diana* (1708, Louvre).

Milo of Crotone, by Pierre Puget. Marble, 1673–1682. The dramatic power of this group for the Versailles gardens contrasts with the calm classicism of other contemporary pieces. Louvre, Paris. (Photo Giraudon)

18th CENTURY FRANCE

During the first half of the century, baroque, previously suppressed, now fought openly with classicism for supremacy.

baroque

The three Adam brothers were staunch exponents of baroque. The eldest, Lambert-Sigisbert (1700–1759), made the theatrical style triumphant at Versailles by installing his *Neptune and Amphitrite* group in the Neptune ornamental pool (1735–1740).

Michel Ange Slodtz (1705–1764) executed in 1753 the *Tomb of Curate Languet de Gergy* in Paris' Saint Sulpice church in the same spirit. Its rather pompous and theatrical style led the leading classicist, François Boucher, to exclaim: "Go ahead and take a look—you'll have a good laugh."

The Lemoynes, father and son (Jean Louis and Jean Baptiste), won renown mainly for their portrait busts. They had a rather exaggerated taste for sculptural realism and preferred to work with softer-than-marble materials (such as terra-cotta, plaster, etc.), which enabled them to capture the most fleeting expressions.

classicism

Edmé Boucharndon (1698–1762) remained a loyal defender of classicism against French rococo and Italian baroque. He continued the traditions of elegance, realism and antiquity. A balance between the two conflicting schools in the early 18th century was struck by two sculptors who in their early years had worked for Madame de Pompadour: Pigalle and Falconet.

Jean Baptiste Pigalle (1714–1785) looked for strength—in contrast to Falconet's over-obvious elegance. Both sculptors combined a real respect for antiquity with a desire to give statues life and movement. Nevertheless, their realism is moderated by a concern for elegance and worldliness, and a striving after purity of volumes inscribed by arabesques.

Etienne Falconet (1716–1791) was famous for his charming statues of bathing

women and children, as well as for his handsome Saint Petersburg (Leningrad) equestrian *Peter the Great,* commissioned by Empress Catherine II of Russia and executed between 1766 and 1778.

Of the many pupils of these two masters, the most important was Augustin Pajou (1730–1809), Louis XVI's official sculptor. Ignoring the almost overwhelming affectation of his contemporaries, he executed many fine portrait busts of women and was responsible for decorating the Opera House at Versailles.

Jean Antoine Houdon (1741–1828), after a period in Rome where he executed the celebrated *Flayed Man,* returned to Paris in 1769 to find all the official positions already filled. Consequently he was obliged to depend on foreign and private clients for his commissions. The result was a wonderful series of portrait

busts, as well as a few huge pieces like the bronze *Diana* purchased by Catherine II of Russia in 1790. Easily the foremost 18th century portrait sculptor, Houdon was so successful that in 1785 he was called to the United States to prepare a model for his famous statue of George Washington now in the Capitol at Richmond, Va. (along with one of his busts of Lafayette). While in America he did busts of several other notable Americans, including Thomas Jefferson.

Voltaire, by J. B. Pigalle. Marble, 1776. Heroic nudity was the sculptor's aim here. Institute Library, Paris. (Photo Giraudon)

Alexandre Brongniart, by Jean Antoine Houdon. Marble, 1777. Houdon's goal in this child's bust was to "keep the truth of the forms." Louvre, Paris. (Photo Giraudon)

17th AND 18th CENTURIES IN ITALY

At the start of the 17th century Italian art was still strongly marked by Giambologna's mannerism, but thanks to Bernini it soon developed into baroque.

baroque art

Baroque art, essentially a reflection of the Counter-Reformation, concentrated mainly on opulent effects, optical illusions and a theatricality in which realism merged with the loftiest spiritual values. Like classic art, it drew inspiration from poetry and mysticism, but its aim was more to stir up feelings than to calm them.

Italian pre-baroque art of the early 17th century is best represented by Francesco Mocchi (1580–1654) and Stefano Maderna (1576–1636). The latter's reclining statue of *Saint Cecilia* in Rome's church of the same name (executed about 1600), with its simple sentimentality, served for many years as a model for all other statues of martyrs. According to a famous chronicler of the times, it was a "marble record of the rediscovery of the saint's bones."

Saint Cecilia, by Stefano Maderna. Marble, 1680. Church of Santa Cecilia in Trastevere, Rome. (Photo Boudot-Lamotte)

Bernini

True baroque art burst onto the world with Bernini.

Giovanni Lorenzo Bernini (1598–1680) was the son of a Florentine sculptor who in 1605 had settled in Rome. So towering and multi-faceted were his talents that, like Michelangelo before him, he dwarfed all his contemporaries and excelled simultaneously in architecture, painting and sculpture. As a young man he executed for his favourite patron, Cardinal Scipio Borghese, four statues, one of which was the famous *Aeneas and Anchises* (1618–1624). In this group, the two reclining figures are carved in the mannerist tradition but curl around a vertical axis in what the Italians were fond of calling a "figura serpentina." Bernini thus created a type of statue which took its cue from antiquity, contemporary mysticism and the doctrines of the Bolognese school. Usually he chose to portray action at white heat, and this dramatic ef-

Aeneas and Anchises, by Giovanni Lorenzo Bernini. Marble, 1618–1624. The twisting bodies are a carry-over from the mannerists. Borghese Gallery, Rome. (Photo Alinari-Giraudon)

fect was heightened by the use of extreme realism in details and by a variety of finishes in the same statue. His famous *David* (1623, Borghese Gallery) seems to hurtle through space because of the violence of its movement.

Bernini's religious works, including his *Saint Theresa in Ecstasy* (1645–1652) in Rome's Carmaro chapel of Santa Maria della Vittoria,

epitomize 17th century religious fervour, whose mysticism very nearly approached sensuality.

A true originality sparks all Bernini's works. His *Constantine* for the Vatican represented a new departure in equestrian statues, while his tombs for Popes Urban VIII and Alexander VII in Saint Peter's were passionate baroque versions of the Florentine tombs originated by Michelangelo. The deliberate showiness of these works stems from the daring of their architectural design,

Cardinal Scipio Borghese, by Bernini. Marble, 1632. Borghese Gallery, Rome. (Photo Alinari-Giraudon)

the use of polychrome marble and bronze and the sense of violence given the whole.

Similarly, Bernini's free treatment of hair, facial features and draperies in his portrait busts gives to these the stop-motion quality of high-speed photographs. A bust of the artist's mistress, Costanza Bonarelli (1625, Bargello Museum, Florence), gloriously

bears witness to this daring technique and realistic artistic concept.

Adulated in Rome, where he usually carried on several projects at once, Bernini's only failure was a diplomatic one—his trip to France in 1665. Yet even this resulted in the equestrian statue of Louis XIV, later remodeled by Girardon, and the marvelous portrait bust of the Sun King now gracing Versailles.

A horde of pupils came and went through Bernini's studio, but none seemed able to escape the shadow of his

Saint Theresa in Ecstasy, by Bernini. Marble, 1645–1652. One of the summits of baroque sculpture. Church of Santa Maria della Vittoria, Rome. (Photo Anderson-Giraudon)

overwhelming personality. Indeed, Bernini had but one rival worthy of the name, Alessandro Algardi.

Alessandro Algardi (1595–1664) first settled in Rome in 1625. Though fascinated by Bernini's style he remained faithful to antiquity and the mannerism of the Bologna school. His portrait busts reflect permanent facets of his sitters' personalities—unlike Bernini's fleeting expressions of mood. Typically Algardi is the bust of Pamphilio Pamphili executed around 1644 and now in Rome's Palazzo Doria. The same sobriety and simplicity may be found in Algardi's tombs, such as that of Leo XI in Saint Peter's, Rome. The Italian also invented a new type of sculpture in his huge bas-relief of *Pope Leo I Meeting Attila* (1646–1653), also in Saint Peter's. Though classic in composition and exceedingly simple, it contains many baroque elements.

Pope Leo I Meeting Attila, by Alessandro Algardi. Marble, 1646-1653. This motion-packed work reveals many similarities with Renaissance bas-relief. Saint Peter's, Rome. (Photo Scala)

Bernini's successors

Seventeenth century Italian sculptural activity centered in Rome, with Bernini and Algardi naturally the leading lights. They exerted a formidable influence over other artists, the most popular of whom were two Italians, Antonio Raggi (1624–1686) and Ercole Ferrata (1610–1686), and the Flemish François Duquesnoy (1594–1643).

Gradually, with the Roman studios reigning supreme, Italian baroque sculpture became evermore elegant and refined, reflecting a kind of preciousness and an extreme sensitivity. At times the virtuosity used in the treatment of drapery far outweighed any anatomical consideration; both inspiration and execution dwindled into mannered frivolity, which was ideally suited to decorating the rather theatrical architecture of the time.

Toward the end of the 17th century and at the beginning of the 18th, some of Bernini's successors carried their mentor's noticeable exaggerations to a deplorable extreme. This particularly applied to Camillo Rusconi (1658–1728), Pietro Bracci (1700–1773) and Philippo della Valle (1696–1770). These Roman artists' immoderation resulted in laboriously complicated works which, despite their technical skill, often border on the ridiculous. Francesco Queirolo of Genoa (1704–1762), responsible for *Illusion Unveiled* (see page 199), was among the more ludicrous perpetrators of such outrages.

Around mid-18th century, a renewed interest in antiquity brought a sobering note which produced more simplicity in sculpture. The tendency, starting with Innocenzo Spinazzi, a Roman who worked in Florence, culminated in Antonio Canova's late 18th century neoclassicism.

In the last half of the 18th century Rome lost her leadership. Sculptors were handicapped by patrons' preference for Greek or Roman originals or copies over newly commissioned works. Orders became few and far between.

The Annunciation, by Philippo della Valle. Marble, 1750. This baroque artist was also influenced by his French contemporaries. San Ignazio, Rome. (Photo Scala)

toward rococo

Piedmont had never been noted for sculpture, and the great architect Juvara had to call on a Tuscan, Cametti, to decorate his magnificent Superga basilica near Turin. Genoa was, however, productive, perhaps because of the proximity of the Carrara marble quarries, and the Frenchman Puget spent several seasons there studying under Algardi. Other prominent Genoa sculptors were the Schiaffino family, of whom Francesco was responsible for the highly picturesque *Rape of Proserpine* in Turin's royal palace.

In Florence, where mannerism reigned and baroque counted for little, the leading sculptor of the day was Innocenzo Spinazzi (1720–1795). While he showed a mild tendency to classicism, as exemplified by the simple altar and urn of his tomb for Machiavelli, Spinazzi could also give full vent to his extraordinary technical brilliance in such works as *Faith* in Florence's Pazzi chapel. Representing a woman whose face and body are entirely veiled, the figure's outline may be barely discerned beneath the cleverly executed folds of drapery.

Rococo predominated in southern Italy where Spanish influence outshone French. In Naples, Francesco Queirolo (1704–1762) carved an extraordinary *Man Escaping the Web of Error* for the San Severo chapel. Here technical extravagance blends with allegorical absurdity. Giacomo Serpotta (1656–1732), working mostly as a decorator in stucco, concentrated in Palermo on chubby-cheeked cupids in a diminished baroque style which contained the seeds of neoclassicism.

Between 1750 and 1770 Italian baroque slowly descended into the depths of rococo, and it took the neoclassicist Canova to revive Italian sculpture and inspire it with new forms and energy.

Saint Suzanne, by François Duquesnoy. Marble, 1629. Santa Maria de Loreto, Rome. (Photo Anderson-Giraudon)

Flanders

Flemish sculpture of the 17th century was much influenced by Italian baroque and by Rubens, whose opulent paintings overflowed with lush forms and vigour. Brussels, Antwerp, Malines and Liège were the main sculpture hubs, and wood the favourite material, being lavishly used in the decoration of confessionals and church pulpits.

François Duquesnoy (1594–1642) was the star Flemish sculptor, though he spent a large part of his life in Italy and left much of his work there. An intimate of the French classical painter Poussin, another expatriate in Rome, Duquesnoy carefully studied antique statues. His specialty, children's portraits, earned him the sobriquet "fattore di putti." He also spent some time working with Bernini in Saint Peter's; his own genius gave him the independence to resist the master's passion for baroque. Duquesnoy's master-

piece remains his *Saint Suzanne*, carved for Rome's church of Santa Maria de Loreto—the epitome of tranquil restraint.

Artus Quellin the Elder (1609–1668), who studied under Duquesnoy in Rome, later returned to his native Antwerp to decorate churches. A classicist like his teacher, he too was to found a long line of brilliant sculptors.

Two other sculpting families, the Verwoorts and the Verbruggens, also worked in Antwerp, where they were famed for their Flemish baroque confessionals. In

Detail from the Pulpit of Saint Rombaut, Malines, by Michel Verwoort the Elder. Wood. (Photo Boudot-Lamotte)

considering this art form, the comment of a critic, P. Fierens, may be worth repeating: "The lacy nature of Flemish baroque, the freedom, fantasy and generosity of its decoration, are in a way an extension of the flamboyant style, and regardless of its transalpine origins Flemish baroque should be considered a native product."

Luc Faidherbe (1617–1697), a native of Malines and both architect and sculptor, studied

Tomb of Archbishop Antoine Cruesen, by Luc Faidherbe. Marble, 17th century. Church of Saint Rombaut, Malines. (Photo J. P. Vieil)

under Rubens in Antwerp for three years. Often his carved works are three-dimensional transpositions of the master's paintings. The Rubens influence also can be seen in Faidherbe's many tombs, which follow the general lines popular at that time throughout Flanders—a cenotaph, encased in a chapel flanked by columns or pilasters, in which the figure lies recumbent in the medieval tradition.

Jean Delcour (1627–1707), another scion of a sculptural dynasty, studied in Rome and on his return to his native Liège made good use of what he had learned from Bernini, though at the same time remaining true to Flemish traditions of realism.

Holland

The Dutch school of sculpture was relatively minor since, in contrast to Catholic Flanders, the Protestant Batavian Republic frowned on what it considered "graven images." The only exceptions were funerary monuments.

Rombaut Verhulst (1624–1698), a native of Malines who had settled in Holland, was the only local sculptor of any importance. His tomb of Admiral Tromp in Delft shows that his cultural concepts remained essentially decorative and austere.

the 18th century

During the 18th century Flanders, like the rest of Europe, fell completely under the sway of contemporary French schools.

Laurent Delvaux (1696–1778), trained as a baroque artist, quickly switched to classicism, while his compatriot, **Pierre Verschaffelt** (1710–1793), who emigrated to Mannheim, reversed this process. The flamboyant theatricality of Flemish baroque is quite evident in Verschaffelt's work despite his earlier classical French training under Bouchardon.

Tomb of Admiral Tromp, by Rombaut Verhulst. Marble, 17th century. Delft. (Photo V. D. Reyken)

17th AND 18th CENTURIES IN CENTRAL EUROPE

During the latter half of the 17th century, France overtook Italy as a source of artistic inspiration, and in central Europe at least, architecture easily displaced sculpture.

Prussia

A shining light among 17th century German sculptors, Andreas Schlüter was born in Danzig in 1660 and died at Saint Petersburg in 1714. He worked almost exclusively in Prussia, his work combining the forms of French classicism with the moderate baroque spirit exemplified by the French sculptor Puget. Among Schlüter's major works is the fine series of *Masks* for the Berlin Arsenal; here the moving, agonized faces of wounded and dying soldiers contrast sharply with the gaudy trophies and symbols of victory surrounding them.

Between 1698 and 1703, Andreas Schlüter executed for Berlin a magnificent equestrian bronze of the Grand Elector Frederick William which can be compared only to the similar piece of Louis XIV that Girardon had made for Paris' Place Vendôme.

Dying Warrior, by Andreas Schlüter. Mask from the Berlin Arsenal. Stone. (Photo Boudot-Lamotte)

French influence being predominant during the reign of Frederick the Great (1712–1786), the king had his palace decorations made in Paris by French artists. In addition, he invited many French sculptors to Berlin, with the result that François-Gaspard Adam, Clodion, and Tassaert (Flemish by birth but French by training) worked for some time in the Prussian capital.

So ardent was Frederick the Great's love for all things French that he started a whole collection of French art, buying sculpted works by Pigalle and Falconet.

Prussian sculpture developed in contact with these French contributions, and before the advent of neo-classicism, culminated in the works of Gottfried Schadow (1764–

Love About to Shoot a Dart, by Nicolas Gillet. The Frenchman Gillet had a great influence in Russia. Louvre, Paris. (Photo Giraudon)

1850). At first strongly influenced by French rococo, his initial exuberance was later tempered by the classical severity which swept Europe in the wake of Napoleon's legions.

Austria

While French classicism conquered Prussia, thanks to Schlüter and Frederick the Great, Italian baroque reigned supreme in southern Germany and Austria.

Balthazar Permoser (1650–1732) was the leading exponent of this mixed Italian-German form of baroque.

Trained in Pietro de Cortone's Florentine studio, he plied his trade mainly in Dresden. A well-known work of his, now in Vienna's Belvedere Museum, is the extremely theatrical *Apotheosis of Prince Eugene of Savoy* (1721), celebrated Austrian general. Balthazar Permoser was also responsible for most of the sculpture on the amazing Zwinger Pavilion in Dresden, whose cornice is held up by wildly gesticulating Amazons.

Georg Raphael Donner (1693–1741), working in Vienna, set out to counterbalance the overdone baroque perpetrated by Permoser, and one of his most delightful and characteristic works is the fountain executed in 1739 for Vienna's New Market. The proportions of this group of lead figures are extremely fine, and the smooth, flowing lines of the women recall the elegant female nudes produced by the School of Fontainebleau and the Italian mannerists. Donner was also responsible for the excellent statues now adorning the Mirabell castle in Salzburg.

Apotheosis of Prince Eugene of Savoy, by Balthazar Permoser. Marble, 1721. Belvedere, Vienna. (Photo Ségalat)

Nymph for the New Market Fountain, Vienna, by Georg Raphael Donner. Bronze, 1739. (Photo Boudot-Lamotte)

southern Germany

Sculptors in the Bavarian capital of Munich remained subservient to Viennese masters throughout the 18th century. Straub, Munich's leading sculptor from 1734 to 1784, was famous mainly for training three outstanding pupils: Ignaz Günther, who magnificently exemplified the charm and mannered grace of German rococo; Boos, who carved highly expressive medallions, and above all Franz Xavier Messerschmidt who, after his apprenticeship in Munich with Straub, worked in Vienna before his final move to Pressburg. It was during this latter period that Messerschmidt executed the delicate series of masks which best illustrate his tormented spirit. These works, some of which are more akin to anatomical studies than artistic endeavour, demonstrate not only the artist's consummate technical skill but his sincere striving for lifelike portraiture.

garden sculpture

It was the heyday of garden sculpture, and German patrons often called in French-trained sculptors for this embellishment. Pierre Verschaffelt (1710–1793), born in Ghent but trained in Paris, Wilhelm Bayer (1729–1797) and Johann Peter Wagner (1739–1809) beautified the gardens of German royal palaces and princely residences with statues similar to those found in the gardens of Versailles but with a limpid grace and tormented elegance sometimes close to rococo.

17th AND 18th CENTURIES IN NORTHERN EUROPE

The Scandinavian countries also took to importing French sculptors. Jacques Saly (1717–1776) traveled to Denmark to execute equestrian statues and busts very similar to those done by his colleagues at home. Edmé Bouchardon's brother, Jean-Philippe (1711–1753), like his compatriot and colleague Larchevêque, became official court sculptor to the king of Sweden.

In Russia, sculpture, prohibited in churches by the Orthodox Church, remained unknown until the 18th century. Then Peter the Great (1672–1725), followed by Catherine the Great (1729–1796), imported foreign artists, including sculptors, from France, Germany and Italy. Peter the Great had summoned to St. Petersburg first Andreas Schlüter, then

Equestrian Statue of Frederick V, by Jacques Saly. Bronze, 1759. Copenhagen. (Photo Sven Thoby)

the Italian Carlo B. Rastrelli. Catherine II called to the Russian capital Nicolas Gillet and Etienne Falconet; the latter in 1766–1778 executed the magnificent equestrian bronze of Peter the Great. Seemingly poised over a cliff, horse and rider beautifully illustrate the fragile balance achieved by contemporary French sculpture between the movement and drive of Italian baroque and the restrained austerity of traditional French classicism.

Equestrian Statue of Peter the Great, by Etienne Falconet. Bronze, 1766–1778. Leningrad. (Photo Boudot-Lamotte)

French sculptors also trained the majority of late 18th century Russian sculptors. Gillet's pupil, Choubine (1740–1805), an acutely observant portraitist, turned out a remarkable series of large busts faithfully depicting most of the notables at the Russian court.

17th AND 18th CENTURIES IN SPAIN

Though some components of Spanish baroque were derived from Italian baroque, the differences between the two art forms are even more striking. Firmly based on native traditions and expressing a religious austerity far more severe than its Italian counterpart, Spanish baroque invariably depicted suffering in its most harrowing aspects, and there was an ever-present mysticism. To this should be added the Spanish taste for colour and for painful realism, as well as the use not only of polychrome but of even different textures and materials. Doll-like moving statues dressed in real clothing were no rarity during this period.

Gregorio Hernández (1570–1636), a Galician who worked mainly in Valladolid, was Spain's first truly baroque sculptor. Typical of highly naturalistic religious works is the *Virgin of Anguish* in Valladolid's Santa Cruz chapel. Enveloped in heavy, brightly hued draperies and weeping glass tears encrusted into the wood of the statue, she immolates herself on a sword: the perfect expression of full-blown Spanish mysticism.

Juan Martinez Montanes (1560–1647), who had definitively established his studio in Seville by the end of the 16th century, closely followed in Gregorio Hernández' footsteps. Like his mentor, he

The Immaculate Conception, detail, by J. M. Montanes. Polychrome wood, about 1630. Seville Cathedral. (Photo Ségalat)

The Virgin of Anguish, detail, by Gregorio Hernández. Polychrome wood, about 1630. Santa Cruz chapel, Valladolid. (Photo J. P. Vieil)

devoted himself almost entirely to religious statues representing the Virgin and saints, escaping this form only long enough to model the equestrian statue of Philip IV now in Madrid's Plaza Mayor. The casting of this piece was actually entrusted to an Italian, Pietro Tacca. Montanes also made many fine statues designed to wear rich clothing, and quite a few with articulated limbs. He is also credited with inventing the "Conception," a type of Virgin which won instant popularity and has changed very little since. In this, the Virgin is shown standing on a crescent moon and surrounded by angels. The earliest of these, it appears, is one dating back to about 1630 which may still be seen in the Seville cathedral.

Alonso Cano (1601–1667) studied sculpture in Seville under Montanes, and then painting under Pacheco, who was mainly responsible for polychroming Montanes' works. Cano himself excelled in both fields and, during a long and adventure-packed life worthy of fiction, managed to travel the length and breadth of his native Spain and dot the country with his prodigious output. One of his finest sculptural

San Juan de Dios, detail, by Alonso Cano. Polychrome wood. Archaeological Museum, Granada (Photo Ségalat)

efforts, the head of *San Juan de Dios* (now in Granada's Archaeological Museum) perfectly illustrates his style, which balances grandeur with tempered realism.

Pedro de Mena (1628–1693) worked for many years under Alonso Cano, and his output reveals a Cano-like balanced inner strength and the same refusal to make concessions to outward shows of emotion. His *Saint Francis of Assisi* in the Toledo cathedral is remarkably simple and pure in line, despite the ultra-realistic treatment of the well-patched homespun monk's robe.

José de Mora (1642–1724), the son of one of Cano's students, continued along the same lines, trying to express mystical emotions through tortured facial expression. His contemporary Luiza Roldan (known as Roldona), daughter of the sculptor Pedro Roldan, succeeded in introducing a fresh note of grace and elegance into this otherwise crushing realism.

Saint Francis of Assisi, by Pedro de Mena. Polychrome wood, about 1663. Expressive intensity compensates for an over-realistic treatment of the drapery. Toledo Cathedral. (Photo Giraudon)

foreign influences

When, toward the start of the 18th century, Louis XIV's grandson acceded to the Spanish throne under the name of Phillip V, Spain was suddenly thrown wide open to foreign influences, first French and later Italian. The new palace of La Granja, besides being designed by French architects, was decorated by Versailles-trained French sculptors, including René Frémin and Jacques Bousseau. Spanish sculpture lost its original, intrinsic traits and the truly native tradition survived only in the

Fountain in the Gardens of La Granja, near Segovia. 18th century. Phillip V called on French sculptors to execute statues and fountains similar to those he had admired at Versailles. (Photo Boudot-Lamotte)

popular arts. In any case, from 1752 onward, the French-inspired San Fernando Academy directed and controlled the country's entire artistic output.

After 1780, the neo-classical tradition which had swept Europe penetrated Spain, without, however, leaving behind anything that might be considered a masterpiece.

17th AND 18th CENTURIES IN PORTUGAL

Portugal's brilliant artistic outpourings of the 16th century seemed to dwindle after her success in throwing out the Spaniards and gaining her independence in 1640. Perhaps the only exception was in the field of elaborately carved and gilded altarpieces, where the exuberant products of the baroque age almost matched the handsome richness of Manueline masterpieces.

During the 18th century, Portugal, like the rest of Europe, was held in thrall by French art with the added influence of a few Italian artists.

Machado de Castro (1732–1822) carved many monumental pieces with heavy swirling drapery, such as those on the Estrella church in Lisbon. His works rather resemble those of his contemporary, Aleijadinho, who after a stint in Brazil produced the rugged prophets adorning the church of Congonhas do Campo.

A special form of sculpture, terra-cotta nativity scenes, suddenly became the vogue toward the end of the 18th century, and some of Portugal's finest talents were bent in this direction. They were highly successful in both Spain and Portugal and represent the acme of Iberian sculptural tradition.

The neo-classical influence which first appeared in Portugal toward 1780 brought no new life to that country's artistic activities and resulted in no important works.

Saint Benedict altar-piece, by Machado de Castro, detail, polychrome wood. (Photo A. Held)

NEO-CLASSICISM

Classical art in all its rigour triumphed in Europe toward the end of the 18th century and beginning of the 19th. Of course this phenomenon was most visible in Italy, always a storehouse of classical remains, but the trend had become intensified with the discovery of Herculaneum in 1711 and the unearthing of Pompeii which began in 1748. The prompters of this new artistic trend, known as neo-classicism, demanded the exact reproduction of the originals since "the ancients have said everything."

Antonio Canova (1757–1822), the foremost Italian sculptor of this school, had to restrain his natural realistic bent in order to achieve the desired purity of expression and form. In a typical work, Canova posed Pauline Borghese as a triumphant Venus (Borghese Gallery, Rome).

Bertel Thorvaldsen (1770–1844), a Dane, competed directly with Canova though his personality was far less forceful. His purity of line won him much praise, and he had

Pauline Borghese as Venus Victorious, by Antonio Canova. Marble, 1804. Borghese Gallery, Rome. (Photo Alinari-Giraudon)

famous statue of a Pilgrim father now standing in New York City's Central Park, as well as in his equestrian and other statues, and many portrait busts. The finest example of Saint-Gaudens' realistic, energetic style is the impressive *Lincoln* in Chicago's Lincoln Park (1887). His other notable works include *The Puritan* (Springfield, Mass.), *Farragut* and *General Sherman* (Madison Square and Central Park, New York City), and the *Shaw Monument* (Boston Common).

wide influence all over Europe and even in America.

In the United States, the Civil War and subsequent change in mores led to the abandonment of neoclassicism in favour of more rugged and realistic tendencies. These are exemplified by John Ward (1830–1910) and Augustus Saint-Gaudens (1848–1907). The former's familiar yet monumental idiom is well illustrated in the

Monument to Lincoln, by Augustus Saint-Gaudens. Stone. In the 19th century, American sculptors preferred powerful realism. Lincoln Park, Chicago. (Photo Chicago Park District)

the contemporary period |

6

Just as new ideas and values enriched 19th century painting with Delacroix and Courbet, so sculpture too underwent a change at this time, though the effect was less forthright and systematic.

Reviving an artistic tradition which had been dormant since the Renaissance, many late 19th and early 20th century painters—Degas, Gaugin, Renoir, Braque, Picasso, Matisse and Derain—also exercised their talents in sculp-

The Cock, by Constantin Brancusi. Gilded bronze. The artist sought simple volume, the pure aspect of the original form. National Museum of Modern Art, Paris. (Photo Ségalat)

ture. In addition, Rodin's dominating personality, technical virtuosity and indifference to official art brought sculpture out of its cocoon once and for all.

Since the beginning of the 20th century, the art world has burgeoned with new ideas, concepts and trends, all helped immeasurably by strongly individualistic personalities. It would be impossible for us to mention every sculptor of worth who is working today, and therefore we have had to limit our comments to a few artists who have pushed sculpture across new thresholds or set out on as yet untrodden territories.

ROMANTICISM

The romantic movement welled up as a protest against neo-classicism. Firmly rejecting antique influences, romanticism tried to convey movement, violent emotion and the picturesque; it drew inspiration from some previously obscure artists of the Middle Ages and High Renaissance. Following closely on the heels of contemporary literary trends, sculpture again became expressive, finally freeing itself from the stifling tenets of neo-classicism, which had degenerated into a dull official academicism.

A marvellously typical romantic work of this period, indeed almost a caricature, is Jehan du Seigneur's *Orlando Furioso* (now in the Louvre), based on Ariosto's famous early Renaissance romance. At the Salon of 1831, the original plaster was instantly acclaimed by the sentimentally inclined audience of the day. Such sculpture won immediate popularity all over Europe but then sadly petered out into pointless, not very interesting genre works. Yet an exception should be made in the case of two men who, though part of the romantic movement, still managed to adhere to the tenets of their early classical training.

Pierre Jean David (1788–1856), a native of Angers, underwent

Orlando Furioso, by Jehan du Seigneur. Bronze. All the violent tendencies of the romantic school appear in this work. Louvre, Paris. (Photo Giraudon)

ROLAND FURIEUX

The Departure of the Volunteers, 1792, better known as *La Marseillaise,* by François Rude. Stone, 1833–1836. Arc de Triomphe, Paris. (Photo Verroust)

the usual classical study, including a long stint in Rome. Soon rebelling against Canova's all-pervasive sway, he was warmly welcomed by the Paris romantic pundits. This extremely prolific young artist specialized in naturalistic, almost scientifically exact portraits, and carved what amounted to an honour roll of France's eminent dashing figures—his public no longer being content with heroes from antiquity.

François Rude (1784–1855) also shed his neo-classical training to combine a direct realism with a talent for movement and graceful poses (as exemplified by such works as his *Little Fisherman* now in the Louvre). His most celebrated opus, however, remains his majestic relief for the Arc de Triomphe in Paris. It shows the departure of the 1792 Revolutionary volunteers. Despite the frenzied activity and exaggerated facial contortions of *La Marseillaise* (1833–1836), as this work is now known, its basic composition remains quite simple and the execution of both bodies and drapery fairly restrained.

FORERUNNERS OF THE MODERN MOVEMENT

Honoré Daumier (1808–1879), best known for his engravings and lithographs, did not take chisel in hand until the age of 26, yet his first busts caused Balzac to declare that he saw something of Michelangelo in them. Wanting no part of contemporary romantic aesthetics, Daumier instead sought a form of precise realism that would reveal his subject's underlying psychology. His expressionism was further heightened by the violence and speed of his modelling, which was not to be equalled until Rodin.

Daumier must be considered one of the standard-bearers of modern art—the man who freed Western sculpture from stale and hackneyed custom. His deeply dedicated political views caused him to be persecuted under the Second Empire. But he still continued to concentrate on truthful renderings of simple subjects. Invariably his art reflected the inherent tragic facets of human existence.

Jean Baptiste Carpeaux (1827–1875) had a career diametrically opposed to Daumier's. Showered with honours by the Second Empire, Carpeaux was saved only by personal integrity from falling into

Ratapoil, by Honoré Daumier. Bronze, 1849. Daumier's sense of caricature and love of movement make him a romantic. Louvre, Paris (Photo Borel)

the trap of facile academicism. The energetic young artist made the most of his time in Italy studying Michelangelo, and his *Ugolin* of 1859 vividly illustrates the pulsating life that he could breathe into a statue. Carpeaux also carried on the portrait traditions of the 18th century, with his busts reflecting his sitter's character and secret thoughts. Pushing his research still further, Carpeaux combined a portrayal of action with a penetrating observation of nature. Such pieces as *Flora*, *The Dance* and the *Four Corners of the World* fountain scandalized his contemporaries. The outraged bourgeois of Paris singled out *The Dance* for special vituperation, calling it an "ignoble saturnalia" and "an offense to public morality."

The very quality in the works of Daumier and Carpeaux that shocked their fellow citizens is precisely what modern critics appreciate and find most promising for the future. There are direct spiritual links between Daumier and Giacometti or Germaine Richier. The output of today's kinetic sculptors is but the culmination of the trend set by Carpeaux, who was still limited by representational necessities.

The Dance, by J. B. Carpeaux. Stone. The explosive motion of this relief almost frees it from its base. Facade of the Opéra, Paris. (Photo Giraudon)

Jules Dalou (1838-1902) studied under Carpeaux. His sketches show a keen sense of observation and the ability to create interesting forms without getting bogged down in detail. Unfortunately, he went too far in spurning bourgeois academicism, so that his works suffered in the end from the equally obvious evil of trite socialist conformity. The same thing befell the Belgian sculptor Constantin Meunier (1831-1905), who also dedicated himself to glorifying labour.

223

RODIN

Like Michelangelo and Bernini, Auguste Rodin (1840–1917) was one of the "beacons" of Western sculpture. His huge and richly varied body of work has been widely imitated, though the true extent of his influence on different schools of sculpture from the end of the 19th century to the present time remains yet to be fully appraised.

Whereas in painting impressionism was the key period, representing the culmination of figurative painting and the point of departure for modern art, so Rodin's works represent the end product of the classical and romantic traditions, and a prelude to the endeavours of contemporary sculptors.

From his early studies with Barye, Rodin held a profound respect for anatomical detail. He also admired both the balance of Grecian works and the inherent strength of Michelangelo's sculpture. Like Michelangelo, Rodin completedly devoted himself to the goal of translating into stone the tragic grandeur of the human spirit with its always underlying psychological tension.

Gifted with dazzling technical virtuosity, he was even accused by some contemporaries of using direct casts of his model to make *The Age of Brass* (1877). Yet Rodin never let his instinctive realism prevent him from exaggerating or twisting a pose or gesture to give it greater meaning. As he said, he always tried to show inner feeling through muscular tension.

Essentially a humanist who disdained all literary subjects, Rodin portrayed men and women in movement, brimming with life. In his *Walking Man* of 1907, "the opposed position of the legs symbolizes a time differential, a contrast between the future and the past based on a theory of motion which he frequently used in his sculpture" (Jean Setz). Among Rodin's most famous works we might mention the *Bourgeois of Calais* (see page 15), *The Kiss* (cover), and the masterpiece, *The Gate of Hell.*

Balzac, by Auguste Rodin. Bronze, 1893–1897. This statue provoked a scandal and was rejected by the literary society that had commissioned it. Paris. (Photo S. Vaucher)

Rodin's contemporaries

Though Rodin had no direct pupils, many artists visited his studio. Among them were:

Charles Despiau (1874–1946), a highly popular portraitist.

François Pompon (1855–1933), who spent fifteen years carving stone for Rodin before becoming a master of animal sculpture in his own right (*The Polar Bear*, 1922).

Antoine Bourdelle (1861–1929), despite a solid admiration for Rodin, gave his works a romantic twist and monumental dimension quite unlike the master's products (*Miner's Monument*, Montceau-les-Mines; *Monument to General Alvear*, Buenos Aires). He also treated classic subjects (*Dying Centaur*, *Penelope*).

Rodin's influence outside France can be seen in the works of the Belgian sculptor Rik Wouters (1882–1916), whose *Mad Virgin* (1912, now in Antwerp's Beaux Arts Museum) reveals that its author—like Degas a few years before—sought to capture the fleeting instant. Max Klinger (1857–1920) in Germany and Charles Malfray (1887–1940) in France show the impact of Rodin.

Hercules the Archer, by Antoine Bourdelle. Gilded bronze, 1909. A work recalling ancient Greek sculpture. National Museum of Modern Art, Paris. (Photo Brogi-Giraudon)

Rodin's successors

Aristide Maillol (1861–1944), whose works are a far cry from Rodin's expressionism, nevertheless resembled the master in respecting classical forms. A Catalan of hermit-like habits, he worked first as a painter and weaver before taking up sculpture at the age of forty, without a shred of formal training. Early on he developed his own style which hardly changed throughout his life. His speciality was the female nude, which he rendered as solid, full volumes composed with architectural exactitude *(Flora,* 1911; *Pomona,* 1912).

The soothing solidity of Maillol's works and their utter lack of literary content link them directly to ancient Greek statues. Maillol had enormous influence on the sculptors of his time.

Wilhelm Lehmbruck (1881–1919) started out as an admiring imitator of Rodin. After a stay in Paris between 1910 and 1914, however, he gradually adopted the pure and static classicism of Maillol, while at the same time leaning toward abstraction. The despair and anxiety visible in his slender, elongated figures reflect a darkening mental state, and he eventually killed himself. German sculpture between the wars learned much from him.

Medardo Rosso (1858–1928), of Italy, started painting at a tender age, then turned to sculpture. His originality stemmed from his pictorial and antispatial concepts. Dazzled by the impressionists' research into the nature of light, he attempted works which could only be seen completely from a single point. "You needn't walk around a statue any more than you need to walk around a form to receive an impression of it," was his dictum. Rosso executed portraits and intimate vignettes of barely sketched-in forms, using broad strokes.

The Mediterranean, by Aristide Maillol. Bronze, 1902–1905. Tuileries Gardens, Paris. (Photo S. Vaucher)

Young Man Seated, by Wilhelm Lehmbruck. Bronze, 1918. Devoid of realism although figurative, this simple, almost barren work exudes an aura of despair and solitude. Kunstmuseum, Duisburg. (Photo Bernd Kirtz)

painter-sculptors

Other early 20th century sculptors drew both inspiration and enthusiasm from the exciting discoveries made in the field of painting.

Gauguin, always attracted to sculpture, revealed a new source of inspiration for contemporary artists—the primitive. Henceforth, the deepening influence of Etruscan, pre-Hellenic and Negro art could be seen in the works of many men who, though essentially painters, also did some sculpture: Derain, Matisse, La Fresnaye, and especially Amedeo Modigliani (1884-1920). The elongated female heads carved by Modigliani are in almost every respect like those he painted. As for Picasso, he started carving masks inspired by Negro art as early as 1905. He later turned to sculpture in the round to produce his huge *Heads* of 1932 and subsequently incorporated a host of materials in his statues *(Man with a Sheep,* 1944).

A lot of painters paved the way to abstraction in sculpture. Two Russians, Vladimir Tatline (1885-1956) and Ivan Pougny (1894-1956) exhibited purely abstract sculpture at the 1915 Saint Petersburg show held by the "suprematist" artists.

The Belgian sculptor Georges Vantongerloo (born 1886), previously a painter and architect, joined the De Stijl (The Style) group and as early as 1917 created "structures in a sphere" which completely broke with all realistic forms.

CUBISM AND FUTURISM

Cubism was essentially a painters' movement. Cubists loved objects for the sake of the object and its underlying structure, and they tried to bring out on a canvas's two-dimensional surface what the eye normally could not find in a classical work. Through his imagination the viewer was thus enabled to perceive the essential whole of the subject treated. Naturally, sculptors were attracted by cubist concepts.

Alexander Archipenko (1887–1964), a native of Kiev, became a cubist shortly after his arrival in Paris in 1908. His first cubist sculpture, in which empty space was accorded a major role, went much further than the simple reconstruction of a figure by means of prisms, cubes or broad, flat surfaces.

Three sculptors from Eastern Europe and two Frenchmen, all working in Paris, led the vanguard of the cubist school of sculpture. Joseph Csaky was born in Hungary in 1888, Jacques Lipchitz was Lithuanian and Ossip Zadkine a Russian. The Frenchmen were Raymond Duchamp-Villon and Henri Laurens.

Woman Walking, by Archipenko. Bronze, 1912. Forms and abstract spaces create the illusion of movement. Saarbrücken Museum. (Photo Archipenko)

Jacques Lipchitz (b. 1891) rejected figures and objects, concentrating on plastic values and tending toward completely abstract sculpture.

Ossip Zadkine (1890–1967), on the other hand, left a body of work marked by the artist's personal lyricism. His passion for figurative expressionism diverted him from the temptations of purely abstract art.

Raymond Duchamp-Villon (1876–1918) executed works which were cubist in inspiration and in the rigidity of their structure, but whose dynamism made them akin to those of the Italian painter-sculptor Umberto Boccioni.

Henri Laurens (1885–1954) produced a richly varied display of work, whose austerely formal straight lines slowly gave way to an interplay of sinuous curves. Like Archipenko, Laurens favoured polychrome to dampen the contrast of light and shadow and to endow each piece of sculpture with the complete autonomy of a painting. "My purpose in polychroming," he said, "is to give each sculpture its own light."

In the list of cubist sculptors, room must also be made for such artists as Gaudier-Brzeska (1891–1915), Pablo Gargallo (1881–1934), Picasso and La Fresnaye, as the latter two felt no compunction in abandoning brush and canvas for modelling clay.

The cubist creed soon spread to every corner of Europe and resulted in the establishment of many fine local schools of sculpture. The cubist banner was flown in Germany by Rudolph Bellin (b. 1888), in England by American-born Sir Jacob Epstein (1880–1959) and in Czechoslovakia by Gutfreund, Filla and Càpek.

Horse's Head, by Raymond Duchamp-Villon. Bronze, 1914. National Museum of Modern Art, Paris. (Photo Ségalat)

FIGURATIVE SCULPTURE

Throughout the 20th century figurative sculpture maintained a healthy vigour, despite an ever-increasing infiltration by the abstract.

Constantin Brancusi (1876–1957), a Rumanian who settled in Paris in 1904, was a leading light in this field. An admirer of Rodin's and the close friend of many cubists, Brancusi nevertheless remained staunchly figurative and kept his artistic independence during his long life. Whatever his subject— a face, a person, an animal, an object—Brancusi sought always to find its original form, eliminating all superfluous details and accessories and maintaining a precise balance between realism and imagination. To support this aesthetic quest he employed a painstaking and refined technique, polishing and re-polishing his fine-grained materials until they shone.

The key to his works can be found in his own words: "Reality is not in the apparent form of things but in their essence. Assuming this, it is impossible for anyone to express reality by imitating the outward surface of objects."

Julio Gonzalez (1876–1942) arrived in Paris from Spain in 1900, there again meeting Picasso. First a painter, he abandoned this art form after the death of his brother, and took up sculpture only at Brancusi's insistence in 1927. Gonzalez' favourite material was metal, which he attacked with the driving energy of a blacksmith. Al-

La Montserrat, by Julio Gonzalez. Iron, 1937. Stedelijk Museum, Amsterdam.

ternating figurative pieces like his *Montserrat* of 1937 with abstractions like the *Cactus Man* of 1940, he maintained the same expressive verve throughout.

Marino Marini (b. 1901) saw things quite differently, stating in 1935 that "the only truly artistic work is one which finds its source in nature and is then able to abstract and transcend it." Marini concentrated on a limited number of themes: nudes, portraits, and above all his *Horse and Rider*, a subject to which he often returned.

Umberto Boccioni (1882–1916), one of the leaders of Italian futurist painting, tried in his few rare sculptures to give this movement a new means of expression in fixing, according to his own words, "the unique form which expresses its continuity in space."

Alberto Giacometti (1901–1966), whose early works are filled with imaginary fanciful creatures derived from surrealism, remarked that "art is perfect hallucination." A native of Switzerland, he sought to re-establish the relationship of the figure in space and thus enable his viewers to grasp the subject as a whole.

Drawing, painting and modelling with equal vigour, from 1946 on Giacometti created a world of haggard emaciated figures, some tiny, some outsized, whose agonized expressions reflect the existentionalist ethos of his time.

Unique Form of Continuity in Space, by Umberto Boccioni, 1913, bronze. One of the rare examples of this artist's work still extant, it ideally illustrates the manifesto on futurist sculpture published by Boccioni in 1912. Gallery of Modern Art, Milan. (Photo Scala)

Silhouette at Rest, by Henry Moore. Travertine marble, 1957. Simultaneously figurative and abstract, Moore harmonizes the proportions of his volumes with surrounding space. Unesco Gardens, Paris. (Photo Massin)

Germaine Richier (1904–1959) was one of the few animal sculptors working in a modern idiom. Giving monumental proportions to the smallest insect, she combined this deliberate distortion with a warm love of nature. She succeeded in mixing the animal and vegetable kingdoms to make an imaginary world whose weird atmosphere and menace is accentuated by her nervous, piecemeal modelling.

Henry Moore (b. 1898) of England has remained faithful to the humanist view of art, but alternates between a figurative and abstract idiom in treating his favourite subject—the reclining human figure. His monumental effigies reveal their true meaning only when seen in the open air, where their rhythm can harmonize with a rural or architectural setting.

Fritz Wotruba, born in Austria in 1907, has emulated Henry Moore in using abstraction to produce works in which the human body "is present at the beginning of the work, and is still there at the end."

ABSTRACT SCULPTURE

Most artists arrived at abstract sculpture through the natural development of their thinking or work. In order to realize both the scope of this art form and the variety of its potentialities, we will consider five artists, all with radically different ideas.

The **Pevsner Brothers, Anton** (1886–1962) and **Naum** (b. 1890), better known as **Naum Gabo,** achieved similar results although pursuing their researches quite independent-

Dynamic Projection at 30°, by Anton Pevsner. Bronze, 1950. National Museum of Modern Art, Paris. (Photo Ségalat)

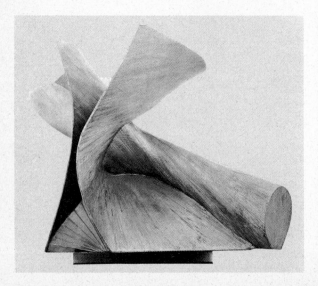

ly. In 1920 they jointly published the famous Moscow Manifesto proclaiming that art should be based on space and time, and that space should become an integral part of any work. Hence the principle of the active void and the elimination of volume in favour of depth, transparency and the interplay of light and shadow. In Anton Pevsner's work, based on interlocking lines and planes, empty space was as essential as solid volumes. It carries to a logical conclusion the revolutionary ideas launched in 1920. The same may be said of Naum Gabo's constructivist sculptures, which are nonetheless quite different from his brother's. It was Gabo who made the first kinetic sculpture: a mechanized knife which carved out an imaginary volume in empty space (1920).

Jean Arp (1887–1966), after his initial training as a painter, participated in many artistic crusades. They included the Blaue Reiter movement in Munich, where he met the Russian painter Kandinsky, and the dada movement that he helped start in 1916 in Zurich. It was at that time that he made his first polychrome abstract reliefs. There is no direct connection between real-life forms and these intertwining round volumes, yet Arp's art seems natural in its innocent poetry and in his insistence on pure formal beauty. He called some of his works "concretions."

Alexander Calder, born in Philadelphia in 1898, the son and grandson of sculptors, studied engineering and pursued a variety of trades before joining the *Abstraction Creation* group in Paris in 1931. His first mobiles, which he called "moving Mondrians," were essentially painted metal plates hanging from wires. The American poured all his talent into producing these mobiles which, moved by air currents, abolish precise notions of space and time, and require for their creation the melding of all the qualities of technician and poet that are Calder's.

Nicolas Schöffer (born in 1912) translated Mondrian's structural principles into three-dimensional forms. In 1848 he created "spatio-dynamism," a concept which involves motor-driven structures put into pre-planned motion. Carrying his kinetic researches a step further, Schöffer then created "lumino-dynamism," in which light was added to the interplay of form and motion.

CONCLUSION

While Paris was the birthplace of modern art and still remains one of its centres, other equally important schools have arisen since World War I in different lands, mainly in London and New York. The American school has been particularly active and inventive. John Storrs (1885–1956), a student of Rodin who first exhibited in 1920, pioneered abstract sculpture in the United States. A later group of artists like David Smith, David von Schlegell and George Segal translated into traditional forms the anguish and growing pains of a new society. Last in this line is Claes Oldenburg (b. 1929), the pop sculptor whose works reveal a continual quest for still more technical and aesthetic freedom.

Modern sculptors may also be painters, engravers, decorators, ceramicists, goldsmiths or architects. Examples of this versatility are Braque, Picasso and Le Corbusier. And whatever aesthetic theories artists may adhere to in this stage of artistic upheaval, they tend to combine painting and sculpture—the Frenchman Jean Dubuffet (b. 1901) and the American Robert Rauschenberg (b. 1925), for example.

Furthermore, at the same time that they utilize traditional materials and techniques, 20th century sculptors have tended to take up strange materials—aluminium, plastics, polyester resins, industrial waste and manufactured articles. Fascinated by recent discoveries, they have invented original techniques whose possibilities seem almost endless—for instance, the use of electronic lighting circuits. Though the form in space remains the basis of all sculpture, the new idea of "environment" has gained ground, and sculpture has now started to move, with sonic and luminous effects added to give it deeper meaning.

Modern sculpture has marvellously reclaimed a field which in the 19th century was relegated mostly to mediocre practitioners of obsolete academicism. Today the sculptor's art is considered an integral part of architecture and of city planning.

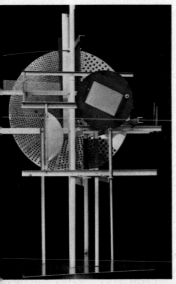

Mobile, by Alexander Calder. 1932. The originator of mobiles, Calder used his imagination to create infinite formal variations. Maeght Gallery, Paris.

Spatio-dynamic sculpture, by Nicolas Schöffer. In spatio-dynamism, motors give sculpture movement. National Museum of Modern Art, Paris. (Photo Ségalat)